THE COMPLETE IDIOT'S GUIDE® TO

Peer Pressure

for Teens

Hilary Cherniss and Sara Jane Sluke

ALPHA

A Pearson Education Company

Copyright © 2002 by Hilary Cherniss and Sara Jane Sluke

International Standard Book Number: 0-02864215-5
Library of Congress Catalog Card Number: 2001092303

04   03   02   8   7   6   5   4   3   2   1

Interpretation of the printing code: The rightmost number of the first series of numbers is the year of the book's printing; the rightmost number of the second series of numbers is the number of the book's printing. For example, a printing code of 02-1 shows that the first printing occurred in 2002.

Printed in the United States of America

Note: This publication contains the opinions and ideas of its authors. It is intended to provide helpful and informative material on the subject matter covered. It is sold with the understanding that the authors and publisher are not engaged in rendering professional services in the book. If the reader requires personal assistance or advice, a competent professional should be consulted.

The authors and publisher specifically disclaim any responsibility for any liability, loss, or risk, personal or otherwise, which is incurred as a consequence, directly or indirectly, of the use and application of any of the contents of this book.

Publisher: Marie Butler-Knight
Product Manager: Phil Kitchel
Managing Editor: Jennifer Chisholm
Acquisitions Editor: Randy Ladenhein-Gil
Development Editor: Deborah S. Romaine
Production Editor: Billy Fields
Copy Editor: Krista Hansing
Illustrator: Jody P. Schaeffer
Cover Designer: Dan Armstrong
Book Designer: Trina Wurst
Layout/Proofreading: Angela Calvert, Mary Hunt, Kimberly Tucker

Contents at a Glance

Contents

Introduction

It Ain't Easy Being Teen

Adults talk to teens about peer pressure all the time. They say to be careful, stand strong, and "just say no." That's all great advice, but we know it's not always that simple. Teen life is complicated, tumultuous, and stressful. Your heads are full of new ideas and old thoughts as you teeter on the fence that separates adults from kids.

Are You Feeling the Pressure?

You're growing up, but you're not sure how you feel about it. All teens experience turmoil; they just deal with it differently. Certain insecure teens put pressure on their peers, influencing them to do things that they don't want to do or wouldn't have done on their own. Teens cave, wanting to be liked or to blend in with the group or at least to be left alone. But, peer pressure isn't always bad. It can influence you in great ways, opening you up to new worlds and inspiring you to take chances.

There are lots of productive ways to handle positive and negative peer pressure. It takes confidence, maturity, and a little know-how. Read this book through to the end. It'll help you understand why peer pressure happens and prepare you to deal with all the crazy, intense situations you're bound to find yourself in at one time or another. You'll thank us for it later.

What We've Got Inside

The Complete Idiot's Guide to Peer Pressure for Teens is broken up into four sections. Each one delves into a different aspect of peer pressure, and the chapters within place that aspect under a microscope. Here's what you find when you peer inside.

Part 1, "The Peer Pressure Squeeze": Growing up is not easy, and you certainly didn't anticipate all the bumps in the road. In Chapter 1, "Teens, Tension, and Turmoil," we define what peer pressure exactly is and show you how it follows you right into adulthood. Chapter 2, "Raging Hormones and Blossoming Bodies:

Growing Up and Growing Out," examines the changes that are rocking your body and your mind. They're new and they're rough, and they're different than anything your parents had to go through.

Part 2, "The Importance of Looking Cool": We've all heard that what you see is what you get, and this section is all about putting your best foot forward. In Chapter 3, "Judging a Book By Its Cover," we'll check out the surface stuff, such as the way you look, the way you dress, and the things you spend your money on. Chapter 4, "High School Hierarchy," goes inside those hallowed hallways to examine cliques and what makes them click.

Part 3, "The Challenge to Act Cool": You alone are in control of how you behave. This section weighs the good, the bad, and the ugly of teenage actions. Chapter 5, "Do Unto Others," looks at the way teens treat one another during these rocky years. In Chapter 6, "Rebel Yell," we focus on your attitude, both at home and at school. Sometimes it's stellar and sometimes it stinks. Chapter 7, "Getting It On or Putting It Off," is all about sex. Whether you should or you shouldn't is all up to you, and here's where we discuss the facts. In Chapter 8, "Drinking, Drugs, and Disillusionment," you'll get the hard truth about these dangerous substances and a no-holds-barred look at how they can destroy your life.

Part 4, "Letting the Air Out: How to Deal with Peer Pressure": This whole peer pressure thing is sometimes so over-whelming that you just want to scream. In this section, we will show you some great ways to beat peer pressure before it beats you. Chapter 9, "Standing Your Ground While Keeping Your Cool," will teach you nifty tricks that you can use to stop peer pressure dead in its tracks. In Chapter 10, "A Gentle Push in the Right Direction," you will discover how peer pressure can be a good thing and how to use it to your advantage. Chapter 11, "Expert Advice: Getting It, Giving It, and Coming Out on Top," will teach you how to help yourself by finding help—and also how to help others by being a leader.

Breaking It Up with Boxes

Open the book, and you're bound to see little boxes chock full of information. Here's what they mean.

Kids with a Clue

Teens just like you talked to us and filled us in on what they're experiencing and how they deal with it.

Pressure Cooker

Danger! Danger! These boxes are filled with warnings about just how scary growing up can be.

Vice Advice

These are some helpful tips that can lighten the load of peer pressure stress.

"He" or "She" Can Be "She" or "He"

We've taken the liberty of randomly choosing one or the other in examples. Most times, we're talking to both sexes, so chances are good that it applies to you. In some obvious times, we are gender-specific, but you're smart and you'll figure it out.

Don't Blame Us—We're Just Writers

Take what we say to heart but not to court. We're just two chicks who have been where you are and made it into adulthood with only a few scars, which we insist give us character. We've checked our facts as best we can, but we're professional writers, so cut us some slack. We don't have advanced degrees, so if you need more than we can give, ask an expert.

Acknowledgments

Hil says: Mom and Dad, my teen years were anything but easy, and at times I wasn't sure we'd make it. But we did, and now it's almost funny. Sari, thank you for following in my footsteps and at the same time showing me the way. Columbus, my little love pig, you make every day better. And Nathan, my handsomino husbanino, how did I ever get lucky enough to find you? You are the best friend and hubby a girl could ask for. I love you MMG!

Sar says: To Mom, Dad, and Stephanie, Thank you for your continuous love and support and for constantly cracking me up. I'm proud to be a part of our family.

We both say: Andree Abecassis, we ladies think you rock! Thanks for your help and your friendship. Randy Ladenheim-Gil at Alpha, thanks for your support and guidance. And Frederick Levy, thanks for getting the ball rolling in the first place.

Trademarks

All terms mentioned in this book that are known to be or are suspected of being trademarks or service marks have been appropriately capitalized. Alpha Books and Pearson Education, Inc. cannot attest to the accuracy of this information. Use of a term in this book should not be regarded as affecting the validity of any trademark or service mark.

The Peer Pressure Squeeze

Whatever happened to that simple life you used to lead? It wasn't long ago that you were carefree and happy-go-lucky, and the sun always seemed to be shining. But times have changed—it's like big, dark storm clouds have suddenly rolled in. These days, life feels like a giant, complicated maze and you're lost in the middle. You are a teenager, stressed out and struggling to meet the demands put on you every day. But don't worry—we're here to help.

The first two chapters of this book take a long, hard look at peer pressure. We'll tell you what it is, why you're feeling it, and how it affects people of all ages. We'll also talk about why you're so touchy and sensitive these days, and how your parents have trouble understanding what you're going through. So, find yourself a comfortable place, grab a frosty soda and some pretzels, and start reading your way to a less-stressed you!

Chapter 1

Teens, Tension, and Turmoil

In This Chapter

- The peer pressure lowdown
- Just being a teen is enough to make you *scream!*
- Fine-tuning your peer pressure radar
- This is just the beginning

Peer pressure is a force to be reckoned with. It's strong, it's powerful, and it's a fact of everyday life for teens. Your life is crazy-hard just dealing with the day-to-day stuff and the physical ups and downs. Throw peer pressure into the mix and wham! It's enough to make your head spin. In this chapter, we'll explain the general facts about peer pressure and the reasons it often feels like you're stuck on a tilt-a-whirl that just won't slow down.

What Is Peer Pressure Anyway?

So now you're a teenager. Finally. But it wasn't so long ago that you were just a little kid playing leapfrog and baking cookies with Mom every day after school. It was a fun life, but the big kids always seemed to have it so much better. They got to do all the good stuff, and no one told them to finish their dinner or take a bath. You just couldn't wait to grow up.

Well, you finally made it. You're taking a monster step toward adulthood. Here you are, a big fancy teenager and life is just peachy keen. It's everything you thought it would be and more, right? Hmmm ... probably not. There sure is a lot more to handle than you could have ever imagined. You're beginning to realize how great it was being a kid when everything was so easy. You faced no real pressures, the sun was always shining, and you didn't even know the meaning of the word *responsibility*. Somehow growing up just isn't the joy ride you thought it would be.

For every year that you blow out another candle on your birthday cake, life gets more complicated. You never know whether you're behaving, looking, or feeling the way you should or the way people expect you to. You feel like you have to keep up with the crowd, which isn't easy when you don't know what you're doing. Suddenly, it's almost like you can't tell who your friends are anymore. Everyone is changing so much that it's hard to recognize even the people you've known forever. You feel all awkward and gawky, and it seems like your classmates are the first to mention anyone's short-comings. They are your peers, and they're piling on the pressure.

Peer pressure is the influence that you feel from your friends and other teens to behave in a way that they will accept. Although sometimes this can guide you on a path to excellence, often it makes you do things that you wouldn't normally do. In the worst cases, it makes you do things that you don't want to do.

This force is insanely powerful. Most people cave in, at least some-times. It's hard to resist pressure that is so super-strong. It's nothing like anything you've ever felt before. It makes that fear of being picked last in kickball seem like child's play. This is the most intense stress you could imagine. It has always been there but not like now.

Peer pressure becomes a huge force at this point in your life because of how important relationships with other people your age are. You want to win the approval of your peers, and often you'll do anything to get it.

Face it: You want to be cool—really cool. Not just mediocre, not just passable, not just okay, but full-blown, all-out, no-doubt-about-it, struttin'-down-the-hallway cool. And who can blame you? Everybody dreams of being that person who everyone else looks up to as the one who does everything the right way. You want to wear the right clothes, have the right hair, say the right things, and just be *that* person. Life would be perfect if that person was you—at least, that's what you think.

Kids with a Clue

"I'm part of the popular crowd, and everyone just assumes my life is so easy, but it's not. It's really hard to have people always looking at you as the cool one. It's like the whole world is waiting for me to mess up."

—Kara, age 17

Most teens are insecure. Try to find even one who isn't. You probably feel unsure of yourself a lot of the time. Sometimes, you might be so wrapped up in your own uncertainty that you don't know how—or even if—you'll ever shake it. But guess what? A lot of people feel way more insecure than you do. Nobody feels great about themselves all the time. Everyone just wants to be liked, to be part of something, to be part of a group. It's important to feel like you fit in, and being accepted by your parents just doesn't cut it anymore. These are some of the feelings that influence people into succumbing to peer pressure.

Being embraced by your peers makes you feel happy and relieved. It's almost like you can exhale after having been so nervous about what everyone else was thinking. You are so glad to be one of the gang. But, remember, it's you, the individual, who makes decisions that will affect you and you alone. It may seem like you and your buddies are one big happy family, but sometimes the choices that you make about how to behave have an impact that forces you to fly solo.

If you get good grades, you can get into college and get a kickin' job. Simple equation. Well, for some crazy reason, smart isn't always perceived as cool in the halls of school. It's not unheard of for students to play down their intelligence—maybe even study less or not answer questions in class that they think are cake. Grades slide. Before you know it, you can't get into the college of your choice— or any college if you really let yourself go. You've graduated, you're going nowhere, and you're alone. That's quite a sacrifice for "cool- ness."

Imagine that you and a couple of buds stop by the drug store after school to buy the new issue of your favorite magazine. Just before you walk in, one of your friends suggests that you each swipe some candy, too. You're all hungry, and you don't have enough cash for the mag and the gummy bears. Mmm, gummy bears. So you all do it. But only you get caught, just as the others are safely out the door. Nobody's coming back to cover for you. Now you have a big black mark on your record, and it wasn't even your idea.

Vice Advice

We all must take responsibility for our own actions. What seems like a good idea at the time—or maybe not all that good, but accepted— could very well end up coming back to bite you. Then, it will be your problem and no one else's.

Unfortunately, doing your own thing is a lot easier said than done. People say all the time that you shouldn't care what other people think. You should make your own decisions and forget about the rest of the world. That sounds good in theory, but in practice it's a whole other story. It does matter what other people think. It does matter that people like you. We all want that—it would be weird if we didn't. But, there are ways to be cool while staying true to your own rules, your own needs, and yourself. You just have to build your strength and confidence, maintain positive relationships with your friends and family, and learn some nifty tricks that will keep you out of trouble and on the right track.

Stressed Out

These days you feel pulled in a million different directions. Why is it that everyone expects something from you? You're not sure what to give, how to give it, or whether you should give anything at all. The pressure of it can be overwhelming. You were never really conscious of your nerves before. You never even knew they were there, but now you feel nervous all the time. With everything that's on your mind, it's hard to know which end is up. The only thing you're sure of is that you're not sure of anything.

You're trying to juggle friends, school, and family and you're afraid that you'll drop all the balls at any second. On top of that, you barely have time for yourself. When are you supposed to fit in the hours to do the stuff that you want to do and that you're interested in? You don't have a magic time machine to stretch out your day. Your schedule is jam-packed and constantly jumbled, and you feel like you're going nuts. Remember: breathe in, breathe out. In, out … aaah. Feel relaxed? Well, enjoy it for the moment because pretty soon something is bound to come up to stress you out all over again.

The strongest force, and probably the one that stresses you out the most, is the ol' peer peeve. By the way, peers are the people your own age at school, in your neighborhood, or wherever. They are an important part of your life. They can share your best times, and if you're lucky, they can help you get through your worst times. The peers who probably have the biggest effect on you are your best friends. But you're also incredibly influenced by the popular kids and the older and bigger kids. If you've got a girlfriend or boyfriend, that person can be another powerful presence in your already chaotic life.

Good friends provide support and a shoulder to cry on. You enjoy a camaraderie, and when you're having fun, there's nothing in the world like it. The obvious bummer is that everyone can't have fun all the time. Your friends can sometimes be annoying. Why is it that you're constantly bickering with some friends while other relationships seem like paradise in comparison? Does that mean that the easy friendships are better than the difficult ones? Maybe but not necessarily. Some combinations of people are just more volatile than others. That could be a good thing though. Often, these are the types of friendships that are the most dynamic because they push you to go that extra mile. But dynamic or not, the friction with these pals can be enough to make you crazy. Your life is suddenly full of drama that you don't like, and you never remember asking for.

Another force that causes you more stress than you'd like to admit is the popular group at school. Maybe you want in, maybe you are in—either way, it's making your life miserable. Individually, the members of the cool clique are more manageable, but together, it sometimes feels like they could move mountains if they wanted to. You don't want to mess with them.

Intimidating as the "in" crowd is, there's nothing more awesome than being considered one of them. If the cool kids like you, forget about it. You're set for life—well, at least until graduation. No matter where you stand in The Great Tower of Coolness at your school, the desire and pressure to be popular can be a definite source of stress.

Under the same category of "things that are awesome one minute and suck the next," you probably also want to add romance. It's fun to want a boyfriend or a girlfriend. It's a blast to have a crush on someone and dream that they will someday be all yours. It's better than chocolate to really truly be in love. It doesn't happen to many people, so if you're one of the chosen few, count your lucky stars—but cross your heart because Cupid is very stingy with those arrows. Even lovebirds are susceptible to the everyday frustrations that plague us all. Often, they are even more affected because of the intense feelings that accompany romance. Every move is magnified, and few people can get under your skin like a significant other.

Sometimes, your honey may even have the nerve to ask for favors or make small demands on you. Like you have all this extra time lying around!

And forget about fights. Whooee, can you two fight. Like cats and dogs, cats and mice, cats and … well, cats. Your sweetie probably drives you so crazy sometimes that you wonder why you keep him or her around at all. A little tiff can make you so angry that you want to run around popping little kids' balloons. Here we go with the drama again. While you're fighting, you can't get your mind off the other person. It's interfering with your schoolwork. Who can focus on geometry when your sweetie could break up with you at any second? Your studies get neglected, your friends get snubbed, and you feel at the mercy of your emotions.

Pressure Cooker

Emotions can be all-encompassing during the teenage years. If not handled with caution, relationships can pass the point of healthy and border on complete consumption.

So what do you do in between stressing out over your friends and your love life? Hopefully you're getting yourself to class. Once there, you have to switch gears, put your game face on, and be a student—and a *good* student at that. You almost feel like a different person in the strange otherworld of the classroom. Five minutes ago you were laughing and cracking jokes with your friends in the hallway, and now you're trying to raise your hand enough times so that you get credit for class participation.

It's no secret that getting good grades is important. You want them, but that isn't enough. You have to work hard for them. You may need them to be allowed to stay on a team or to build up your transcript for when you apply to Dream University. Teachers are all over you, making sure that your homework is done well and that your papers are handed in on time. They have expectations, but can you blame them? Do a good job on an essay question on your first test, and they'll look for the same on every test after that. Talk about pressure!

And do you have older siblings who were good academically? Maybe good athletically? Unfair as it is, teachers and coaches may expect the same from you. Likewise, if your siblings were trouble-makers, teachers may assume the worst of you. You will have to work extra hard to prove that you're on top of your game. You probably do your best to rise to the occasion, but it's not easy. And it's taking up tons of your time.

Aside from school and your peers, pressure comes many other places. Just look to the home front. Your family members and the relationships that you have with them can be comforting, but they can also make you want to hide under your bed. Could they leave you alone for, like, one minute? One minute is all you ask, and they can't even do that. Until recently, it seemed a lot easier to be a member of the family, but now you can't have a normal conversa-tion without getting into some kind of stupid little squabble if not a knock-down, drag-out fight. You're growing apart from them, which is normal.

Unfortunately, it may not be so easy for your mom or dad to take this sudden cutting of the apron strings. They want you to go to Granny's every Sunday, like you always have. It used to be fun. Mmm, apple pie. But now you want to hang with the guys and watch football and eat junk food and have burping contests. Actually, Granny would be mortified if she could see what kind of activity you'd rather do instead of letting her pinch your cheeks all day.

Then, there's the whole thing about living up to what your family expects of you. Since you were born, your parents set the rules, and you followed them. With the exception of sneaking an extra snicker doodle here and there, you rarely broke any of them. Whoa, baby, are the teen years different or what? On one hand, you're rebelling—but on the other hand, you still love your folks and want to please them. Some rules you break while others you know better not to. Here you are feeling split again. It's hard to be everything they want you to be—very hard. They expect good grades, good manners, and good behavior. But how can you do it all? How can anyone do it all?

Kids with a Clue

"My parents expect me to be a starter on the baseball team, work at my uncle's store, do my chores, and still get straight A's. It's impossible to make them happy."

—Jayson, age 15

As if your real life isn't stressful enough, the constant media presence of Hollywood actors and the stars of the music world don't help your ego at all. Catch a flick, turn on the tube, pick up a mag, or flip on the radio, and you'll find them everywhere. You know who they are: the beautiful people. Beautiful, perfect people. Yuck! They're enough to make you want to puke all over their designer outfits.

Lots of the characters in shows and movies are not only beautiful, but they're rich, too. They have the slickest cars, the hippest outfits, and the hundred-dollar haircuts. And they're happy. Not just happy like you get when you pass the test that you forgot to study for. These people are honey-dripping, bird-singing, shiny-happy. Well, except for certain melodramatic soap opera characters—and they're just acting.

How can you possibly compete with this? Seriously, those aerobicized, yoga-ized bodies are not even close to the way most people look. And their teeth are whiter than a boy band. Well, at least you can rest easy knowing that they're bleached. And most of their other perfect parts are equally phony. Remember, these celeb images force you to put totally unrealistic expectations on yourself. You don't have to look like them to be considered cool and attractive. They're mostly fiction not reality.

Sometimes, believe it or not, none of these factors give you as much stress as someone you may not have even considered: you. Yes, it's true, sometimes you can be your own worst enemy. You know that crazy, mixed-up head of yours? The one we've been talking about all along? Often, pressure comes from right inside that seemingly innocent noggin.

Sure, you can blame peers, school, family, and Hollywood for the stress you feel. But others aren't always forcing your hand. They aren't always pushing you to do stuff you don't want to do. Some pressure is self-imposed. True, you are influenced by the world around you, but from there you develop your own ways of thinking. No one has ever actually declared that you should have sex because everyone else is. But you assume this to be true and, therefore, what you should be doing. Last Friday when you walked into that raging house party, no one actually said, "Have a beer. It'll make you feel grown-up." Geez, no one even offered you one. You had to decide for yourself whether to pick one up. This can be quite a difficult choice to make. After all, the pressure that comes from within you may be the strongest of all.

Is This Peer Pressure, or Am I Dreaming?

Peer pressure isn't always a cinch to spot. It takes on many different forms and can be positive or negative. It happens in one way or another almost constantly. Although it surrounds you, it can often be tricky to identify. You may not even realize when it's affecting you.

How can you combat something if you don't even know it's happening? You've got to learn to recognize it. Once you become familiar with some examples, you'll start knowing what to look for. Soon, you'll be able to spot it from a mile away.

Everyone knows they're feeling peer pressure when it's done in an obvious way. How many of these phrases have you heard before?

- "Come on. Everyone's doing it."
- "If you were cool, you'd try it."
- "Be a real friend ...."

- "Don't be such a dork."
- "Afraid your mommy will yell at you?"
- "Oh, grow up."
- "I dare you."
- "You're such a priss."

Cheesy, cheesy, cheesy—every last one of them. Out of context and just written on the page, these words look totally ridiculous. But now adapt them to a conversation you have with someone you know. All of a sudden they have a whole new relevance. Hear them come from the mouth of a girl you look up to and think is cool, or even some guy you're a little scared of, and the words take on a life of their own.

Basically, anytime you hear words that mean anything close to "You're a big loser if you don't 'fill-in-the-blank,'" that's peer pressure. It's a terrible feeling to be targeted with these words. They're extremely negative and also harshly blunt, enough to throw you into a tailspin. Suddenly, you're a deer in headlights, and you may give in mainly because you were blindsided.

Words don't have to be threatening to be powerful. Sometimes, offhand comments can pack a punch of pressure. Teasing and joking often hurt the feelings of the victims. These comments leave behind residual anger and damaged egos. The person hurling the comments may not even realize their impact. Teasing someone about their, shall we say, rather substantial-sized schnoz may drive them to want a nose job even if they never gave their sniffer a second glance before.

Another example of sly peer pressure is being guilted into doing something for someone else. A friend convinces you to drive him to school even though it's out of your way and you really need the time to study. A classmate asks you to help her prepare an oral report. You give in and end up spending more time working on her project than your own.

Kids with a Clue

"My brother says I'm a doormat because I always do what my friends want instead of what I want. I think I'm just being nice."

—Lowell, age 13

Some examples of pressure are even more subtle. Think for a minute about the style of language you use. You may feel like you need to speak a certain way to fit in with the crowd. You won't even notice when words creep into your vocabulary courtesy of your peers. If "everyone" starts using certain lingo, before you know it, you do, too. *Fresh, phat, rad*—there are lots of examples of words that come in and out of style just like clothing. Using a dated word can make you sound out of it. No one wants to be guilty of being "*so* five minutes ago," so you alter your use of language when everybody else does.

It's amazing how you can be influenced by peer pressure and have absolutely no idea it's happening. There are so many forms it can take. We'll go over more of them throughout the book, so read on. We know that it's impossible to be constantly looking for signs of pressure during your daily life. That would be exhausting. But it is good to be aware that it's out there. Pay attention, and you'll start to notice when a comment sounds fishy. This is a good first step to coping with the whole darn peer pressure thing.

It Doesn't End at 20, So Deal with It

This peer pressure stuff is a lot to deal with during a time in your life that's already so tumultuous, right? But it's temporary, it'll get easier as you get older—then by the time you're an adult, it's smooth sailing, right? Sorry, folks, but that couldn't be further from the truth. You may grow out of your teens and away from the peers who surround you now, but the pressure never lets up. Your peers grow older and the pressure comes with them. It's a fact of life at every age. But don't sweat it. If you learn how to deal with it now, resisting it will be a snap—or, at least, less traumatic—for the rest of your life.

Ever hear the phrase "keeping up with the Joneses"? It's an old cliché that refers to Regular Joe's desire and need to constantly compare himself to his neighbor and make sure he's not being out-done. That means having a car just as nice, if not better. If Mr. Jones joins the country club, Joe's head begins to spin and he feels like he should join, too—maybe even run for the board. It's compet-itive, conformist thinking, but, unfortunately, it's a fairly universal truth. The solution seems obvious. If Joe would just concentrate on his own life and stop being so nosy about what the neighbors are up to, he'd be a lot happier and less stressed out. Why would he want to join the country club, anyway? He hates tennis and snooty peo-ple. But it doesn't matter because in the moment he feels the pres-sure.

All adults feel the squeeze—your parents included. Do they keep their lawn mowed? They probably do so that it looks nice and neat, but it's also because everyone else on your block mows theirs, too. How could your parents resist? It would look tacky if they were the only ones with a jungle growing in their front yard. And if all their friends' kids are taking piano lessons, crack your knuckles and find "middle C" because you're next. They feel the influence of their peers, and their actions reflect it.

In the workplace, pressure comes from all angles as well. How does Frank know how to dress appropriately at his new job? He'll look around to see what his co-workers are wearing. And how should he behave during the staff meeting? Casual? Stuffy? Where should he take business associates to lunch? His favorite steak house or the trendy new trattoria? Chances are, he'll check out everyone else and then fall right into stride next to them.

Gramps is gumming his banana pudding with his buddies at the rest home when, all of a sudden, Irving's grandkids drop in for a visit—for the third time this week. You haven't visited Gramps since last month. Irving's kind of snotty anyway, so he drops a slight comment about this to Gramps, which is just enough to send him shuffling to the pay phone. Suddenly you get a call, and he's yelling about how you'd better get your disrespectful butt down to visit 'cause you're making him look like a dang fool! Yup, even at 85, peer pressure is still a force to be reckoned with.

The Least You Need to Know

- Peer pressure is a powerful force that influences you constantly. The desire to fit in is a strong one and can sway you to do things that you don't want to do and maybe shouldn't do.

- The teen years are a busy, stressful time, and it's easy to feel spread thin. Take time to unwind. The person you have the greatest responsibility to is yourself.

- Although peer pressure has many faces, it becomes easier to deal with when you learn how to recognize it.

- Everyone young and old feels peer pressure—even people who seem the most perfect and put together. Remember, you're not alone in your struggle to fit in.

Chapter 2

Raging Hormones and Blossoming Bodies: Growing Up and Growing Out

In This Chapter

- Give me a hug, then get out of my space
- The great hormone surge
- Why is everybody always looking at me?
- That's what friends are for
- Your parents never had it this tough

Do you feel like you woke up one morning and your whole world had turned upside down? When you went to bed the night before, you were a carefree kid without a worry in the world. You were living for the moment. With daylight came anxiety, complexity, and puberty. Who remembers signing on for this?

Welcome to the Teen Years

You never realize how good childhood is until it's gone. Those blissful days are a thing of the past, and lately you find yourself less than thrilled to get out of bed and face the day. You're not sure when or even how it happened, but life suddenly became difficult. You're faced with making decisions way more complicated than whether to trade your tuna sandwich for somebody else's PB&J. And you don't feel ready, willing, or qualified to do it. But you have no choice. You are in the midst of one of the hardest phases of your entire life, and it feels like it's lasting an eternity. But, remember, technically, you are a teenager for only seven years, so consider it just a run of bad luck for some mirror that you probably broke when you kicked a soccer ball in the house and tried to bury the pieces.

How many times do you walk through the hallways at school feeling like you just don't belong? You hope and pray that the floor will miraculously open and swallow you up to relieve you of your agony. Have faith; there is a method to making this problem much easier to deal with. The best way to power through those nerve-wracking moments is to tag-team it and face the crowd with a partner. Remember those hot summer days when you had to swim with a safety buddy? You were each other's lifeline in the pool, and you felt reassured knowing that someone was looking out for you to make sure that you didn't drown. But now sometimes you feel like you're helplessly splashing through those long, daunting high school hallways. Well, with your comrades around you, the trip from math class to English class can be less scary and more like a walk in the park.

While friends are great, sometimes the last thing in the world you want is company. For the first time in your life, you are craving privacy. Your parents want you to keep your bedroom door open, but that only makes you feel suffocated. You desperately want to not only close it but also to lock it, slap on a chain, and get a snarling

pit bull to protect against intruders—namely, *them*. This newfound
need for independence is expected, but make sure not to completely
shut out the world around you. We all need to be social to keep
ourselves sane. There's a reason why a misbehaved prisoner is sent
to solitary confinement. Being trapped alone is the ultimate punishment.

Vice Advice

Teenagers are infamous for their quickly
changing moods that leave them confused
and cranky. If you feel like you need to be surrounded
by people, join your buds and have a ball. If you
want some peace and quiet, slip on your headphones,
take a long walk, and just chill out.

There is no concrete rule as to how much companionship is the
right amount. One minute, you might feel all alone, excluded, or
abandoned. The next, you are feeling smothered by even casual
conversation. You can never perceive which mood is going to strike
when. You just know that whatever you're feeling, it's intense and
confusing and driving you crazy.

Physical Headlines

Mirror, mirror on the wall, who the heck is that? You see your re-
flection, but that person staring back at you is a stranger. Whose
body are you wearing, and what happened to the one you were cozy
in for all those years? Puberty has hit, and it's not a polite little
tap—it's a full-on slap in the face. You feel achy, awkward, and miserable and that's on a good day. Your favorite jeans now wear like a
pair of floods, and your arms dangle spastically from the sleeves of
your sweater. Either you are inches taller, or the doorframes in your
house have sunk. And that desk in your room must have walked

over a few feet because it never got in your way before. Suddenly, you're large—but you are far from in charge.

It's hard to get used to the changes of your new body. Even walking feels weird on those long, untrained legs. Many people have such intense sudden growth spurts that they actually get stretch marks from their skin being pulled. Muscles that you didn't even know you had are being overworked as estrogen and testosterone flood your body, changing your physique from tyke to teenager.

The good news is that you grow only so much and then you get to stop. Your body will settle into itself, and you will once again regain control of it. Her newly swaying hips will fall into step nicely with his confident swagger. Your gawky limbs will fill out, making you strong and powerful. You will feel ready to face the grown-up world with your adult body and take it by storm. So, as much as you might feel like there is an alien inside you commanding your ship with absolute reckless abandon, know that someday soon you will be the captain again.

Kids with a Clue

"It's so weird. One minute I'll be fine, just hanging out with my friends. Then all of a sudden I'm crying hysterically and I don't even know why."

—Vanessa, age 16

Along with growth, puberty packs a double punch by also hitting you with mood swings. Your body is pulsing with hormones that cause you to act in ways that scare your parents almost as much as they confuse you. Simple frustrations like having your foot accidentally stepped on are enough to make a once passive and laid-back guy want to throw a punch and start a brawl. A happy-go-lucky gal who usually has a spunky gleam in her eye might burst into tears for absolutely no reason at all. You may find yourself laughing hysterically and inappropriately when nothing is even remotely funny. You can't stop these crazy highs and lows; you just have to try to gain control of them as best you can. And be forgiving when they happen to your friends.

Emotional Scoop

Your life is now filled with a whole new set of worries. When you were a little kid, if you fell down, you got up. You never considered that the entire school might be watching you, laughing and pointing at your misfortune. My, how things have changed! A little stumble could ruin your entire day. You will spend hours agonizing over who was witness to your klutzy spill and what they must think about you now.

Self-consciousness is like an uninvited guest at a party. Nobody wants it there, but there is no easy way to get rid of it. Suddenly, you are hypersensitive about everything, and you are sure that all the other kids are staring at you, convinced that you are a freak. There is nothing worse than waking up in the morning with a zit on your forehead so big that it needs its own zip code. You can't possibly go to school like that. But before you hide under your covers and play possum, think about your friends and their flaws. How ridiculous would you think they were if a little pimple kept them from going on with their lives. It sounds insane, doesn't it? So, why is it any different for you?

The truth is, it's not. It just feels that way. Everybody is too wrapped up in his or her own insecurities to notice the details about yourself that you obsess over. It may seem like the whole school is staring at you when you walk into the gym to watch the basketball game. You are sure they are all thinking, "What is she doing here?" You want to leave immediately rather than face the crowd. But don't go running anywhere; you're just being paranoid. People are not staring, and most won't even notice you are there. If they do, it's probably because they're happy to see you. It should help to know that most of the faces in that crowd feel the same anxieties you do. You'd never guess it about them, which means that they'd never guess it about you. So grab a seat on the bleachers and have fun. You're all in the same boat.

Aside from your paranoia, do you feel like you're developing quite a track record for screwing stuff up lately? It doesn't matter what it is—you just know that you are definitely going to mess it up. Simple, everyday tasks that you normally take for granted can become daunting, and you are scared to even attempt them for fear that you will fail. When did picking out a pair of shoes become an hour-long agonizing chore? This total lack of confidence may make you feel like you should start sucking your thumb again. For the first time in your life, you are constantly filled with incredible, overwhelming self-doubt.

Kids with a Clue

"The other day I spent an hour and a half trying to decide what I wanted for a snack. I just could not make up my mind. By the time I figured it out, my mom called me for dinner. I'm such a geek."

—Maya, age 14

There always used to be easy answers to questions. Do you want peas? No. Did you like that movie? Yes. Now, suddenly, you can't make a simple decision without changing your mind 50 times. Maybe you want peas but only if you have the chicken. Or should you have the steak? As for that movie, it was okay, but the ending was weak and the middle didn't make much sense, so maybe you didn't really like it all that much. Ugh! You clap your hands over your ears to drown out the inquisition. You want to shout at everybody that you have no idea about anything at all, so please stop asking!

It's bad enough that you're totally confused about what you want to do and who you want to be. But compound that with the fact that others are bound to make old-fashioned assumptions about who they think you should be. "Boys will be boys" is a lame saying that should be buried alongside "A woman's place is in the kitchen."

Who decides the appropriate way a boy should act? What if you are different from the presumed norm? It certainly doesn't make you any less of a boy. It makes you an individual, a person in your own right. So many gender expectations are placed on teens that they can make you doubt yourself for no good reason at all.

Classic gender roles aren't nearly as rigid as they once were, but you still feel their strong influence when you're growing up. From an early age, boys are taught to love sports. They are supposed to wake up in the morning thinking about sports, spend the whole day playing sports, and go to sleep dreaming about sports. For some guys, this is an enjoyable reality, but for plenty of others, it is nothing short of a nightmare. There are so many other things in the world that guys may rather focus on, like music, science, or art. But these interests aren't thought of as what typical manly men like to do. Tough guys hunt, arm wrestle, and spit. Does this mean that you should drop your sax and start hocking loogies? Please don't. It might be hard to be the guy who loves ballet more than basketball, but if you try to fake it, you're denying yourself and fooling nobody.

And what about the gals who find the thought of wearing anything pink worse than the idea of sharing a room with a little brother? They scoff at the rules that girls are supposed to love all things frilly. There may have been a time long ago when the fair young maiden was dainty and delicate, but those days are over. Chicks nowadays can kick butt. Just because you are the girl who would rather watch wrestling then spend a half-hour painting her toenails, you're not any less of a woman.

Kids with a Clue

If you look or act differently than what is expected of your gender, don't worry about it. Nobody is a textbook case. Revel in your individuality and be confident in the fact that there is more to you than what's required.

Some people may never get you. They're called your parents. You know that you look just like your mother, but there are days when you are convinced that you must be adopted. There is no way you could possibly be their offspring. Your relationship with your folks is changing, and you are looking at them with scrutinizing eyes. Not only do they not understand you, but you don't get them either. Did your mom always dress like that? And what's with your dad's comb-over? Who does he think he's kidding? Their mere presence can be humiliating. The last thing you need is to be seen in public with these people. Family night at the movies is a thing of the past, and if you could sit at separate tables at the restaurant so nobody knows you're together, you'd be thrilled.

You're not sure when it happened, but it is blatantly obvious that you're not that interested in what your parents think anymore. When you were a kid, they had all the right answers. You were convinced that your dad was a genius and that your mom was an angel sent down from heaven just for you. These days, you think that your dad is more like a moron and that your mom should sprout horns and carry a pitchfork instead of a purse. You are positive that their only mission in life is to make you miserable. When they try to be nice, it must be an act, and you don't buy it for a second. Sure, they tell you that you're beautiful, but they *have* to say that. They're your parents, it's their job. If they like your new sweater, there must be something wrong with it, and you'll never put it on again.

It might feel like you are supposed to push your parents away in order to gain independence. You feel like you don't need them anymore—they've served their purpose, and you're ready to move on. But don't write them off completely. You feel like a tough guy, but you still need their support both emotionally and financially. And, believe it or not, if they weren't around, you would miss them like crazy. So try and get past all their bizarre little quirks; after all, they are putting forth effort to get past yours. And, years from now, you might just like them again.

Friendship's Not That Simple Anymore

When you were a kid, your pals were important because they were the Marco to your Polo, the Duck-Duck to your Goose. Childhood games are always better in groups—the more, the merrier. Your friends were the kids who lived on your block, and it didn't matter what their interests were. As long as they were willing to play freeze tag and chase the ice cream man, they were good enough for you.

Now that you are older, these pals become more essential. Choosing them has become an art form. You rely on your friends for advice and support when it seems that everything is falling apart around you. It isn't always easy to develop this type of bond. Good friendships take time and need to be cultivated.

It is often easier to become friends with people of the same sex. Inherently, you have more in common with somebody going through the same body and emotional changes that you are. You can compare notes about boobs and body hair with others who are just as shocked and overwhelmed by it as you. Also, girls are big talkers; they love to spend hours rehashing every moment of their day while most guys don't bother to pay attention to the details. Neither way is right or wrong; they're just totally opposite. And, unfortunately, that's not something that changes when you get older. The two sexes never see eye to eye, but that's what makes these relationships so intriguing.

During elementary school recess, one of the most popular games to play was "Catch and Kiss." Everyone would run around and try to catch each other. When you did, you were supposed to kiss. But nobody ever really wanted to smooch, which, looking back, was a major flaw in the game. Girls thought boys had cooties, and boys thought girls were totally gross.

Now that you're older, those same icky people suddenly don't seem so awful. You begin to realize that they could actually be your friends. Guys and girls start to see each other as members of the same species who might be worth giving the time of day to. You may find yourself on the phone for hours on end with a boy you once thought was a hopelessly nerdy goofball. He suddenly seems smart and funny, not to mention kind of cute.

Your friends are now the most important people in your world. You count on them to help you make decisions and figure out how to act, how to dress, and who to hang out with. They have become like a second family to you and are probably a way more substantial part of your life than your parents or your siblings. After all, there is nothing better than wasting the day away with your best bud either watching movies and pigging out or shooting hoops until it's too dark to see the basket.

Parents Just Don't Understand

How many times have you heard your parents say that they understand completely what you are going through? After all, they were your age once. While this is an indisputable fact, life is drastically different these days. In this modern information age, kids are growing up faster and are more aware of the world than their parents ever were.

Information about everything you could ever dream of is accessible through your computer. Log on to the Web, and what do you see? It ain't your mama's Internet, that's for sure. If your parents had a report to write, they had to spend hours in the library doing research from actual books. It sounds archaic compared to the wealth of knowledge at your fingertips. But sometimes too much information can be a bad thing. There are lots of Web sites that are inappropriate for kids, teens, and most adults. And yet, with a simple click of the mouse, there they are, ready to teach a lesson better left untaught.

Internet chat rooms are the new fun place to hang out. In theory, they are a wonderfully convenient invention. You can communicate with people all over the world without racking up a billion-dollar phone bill. By talking to teens from different cultures, you expand your horizons and get the scoop on what's hot in Europe, straight from the source.

Pressure Cooker

Unfortunately, a lot of shady characters prey upon innocent teens and corrupt them through e-mails. When your parents were your age, the rules were simple: Don't talk to strangers. But now, with computers giving everyone anonymity, it's almost impossible to tell who the strangers are. Scary.

The repercussions of sex were also completely different back in that day. When people did the deed, the only thing they really had to worry about was pregnancy and the occasional STD, which could probably be treated with a cream or pill. Nowadays, those fears still linger, but they are magnified. Sex can kill you. If you do it and you're not careful, you could contract HIV, which is a heck of a lot more frightening than anything that your parents' generation had to consider. It makes you wonder if it's even worth it.

Perhaps, the most terrifying thing about being in high school these days is the recent wave of violence. Kids carrying guns to school is a new problem that nobody is equipped to deal with. It used to be that only police officers, hunters, and hardened criminals had guns. Now, you never know who in your French class is packing heat.

School is supposed to be safe. When you leave your parent's house in the morning, you should feel secure that although they might be boring, your classes will protect you from danger. Nobody said it was always easy and fun to be a teenager, but that doesn't give anybody license to pick up a gun and start firing. It's hard to believe that security guards and metal detectors are a part of some students' everyday routine. Your parents never had to deal with that, and it is a shame that you do.

Students in states like Colorado, Kentucky, and California mourn the losses of their friends and teachers. Parents grieve over children's lives cut tragically short. It's a cruel injustice that you have to fear for your life when you walk across campus, but that is the state of affairs these days.

But it doesn't have to be. If you know that another student possesses a gun, don't hesitate to tell an adult. Some twisted kids may believe that packing heat makes them a big shot. The truth is only a loser thinks violence is an answer to their problems. Don't let their guns become your problem. Take a stand, be a hero, and keep your school safe.

The Least You Need to Know

- It's totally normal to feel the need for constant companionship as well as the desire for independence.
- Puberty wreaks havoc on your body and your mind, so get ready for a bumpy road ahead. (But don't worry; the road eventually smoothes out again.)
- Paranoia, insecurity, and humiliation by your folks are par for the course, so try to keep a clear head.
- Friendship is now a complex puzzle that requires time and effort to assemble correctly.
- Your parents were teenagers once, but they didn't have nearly as many complicated scenarios to sidestep as you do. Have patience with them; they're just trying to make sense of it all, too.

The Importance of Looking Cool

Wouldn't it be nice if we could all wear our insides on the outside? All the focus would be on who you really are: your personality, your passions, your pancreas. Maybe then people wouldn't pay as much attention to the superficial stuff.

We live in a time where looks matter—a lot. The first impression people get is your face, your body, your clothes, your car. These next two chapters take a look at looks. What you look like and what you own says a lot about who you are. Who you hang out with can say even more. Popularity is a game we all play whether we like it or not. So, think about who you are and who you want to be when you turn the page and read about perception.

Chapter 3

Judging a Book by Its Cover

In This Chapter

- Everybody speaks a different language
- You are what you own
- That fad is so-o-o five minutes ago
- Assumptions and presumptions: scratching the surface

You'd never guess by looking at them, but there are a lot of punk-rock poets and preppy bad boys. Shocking? Not really. We're all a lot different than we appear on the surface. Unfair as it seems, we are all judged—at least, at first—by how we present ourselves. In this chapter, we'll take a deeper look at physicality, image, and perception.

Body Battles and Hairy Situations

Take a long, hard look in the mirror. Like what you see? Probably not. You may think that your thighs are too fat or that your arms are too scrawny. You would clean your room every day for the rest of your life if you could have the killer curves of that Überbabe in your math class or the chiseled Adonis pecs of the captain of the wrestling team. But just ask them how they feel about their own bodies: The babe probably wishes that her breasts weren't so big, and the wrestler would do anything to be a few inches taller.

Diet and exercise can alter the size and shape of your body. However, genetics is also a very powerful force. Although it's not always easy to drop that extra 5 or 50 pounds, with some hard work and discipline it is doable. But just try changing the thickness of your wrists or the width of your hips. Not easy, we know—we've tried.

We all wish we were born supermodels or star athletes, but, alas, most of us are not even close. It does help to remember how far from the average those babes and hotties are. Although beautiful people stare at us daily from billboards and magazines, they are really the minority. You may feel surrounded by them because of their presence in the media, but that's a big misconception. Just take a walk down the street, and you'll see. In reality, there are very few of them and a lot more of you. Besides, they're not as perfect as they seem. They have lots of help. Makeup artists and fashion consultants work their magic for hours to make models look their best. So cut yourself some slack when flipping through a mag.

Beauty trends change constantly, but thinness has been in vogue for quite a while now. Centuries ago, plumpness was encouraged. It was looked at as a sign of health and vigor, and it gave the impression that a person was well-to-do. However, over time, especially during this past century, the image of what's considered beautiful has changed. The icons of beauty in our society are getting thinner and thinner. The average celebrity body is actually smaller now than it has ever been. Many celebs even look unhealthy. You know the ones, all bony with those spidery arms and lollipop heads. It's weird to think that these are the people we're all supposed to emulate. Bodies like theirs are nearly impossible to attain in a healthy manner, especially for teens who are still growing and changing.

People often assume that the thinner you are, the better your life must be, or that you have to be built to be popular and cool. Even though exterior and interior beauty do not go hand in hand, many people wrongly believe that by changing their bodies, they will become happier. Of course, this is far from true. We all know twiggy people who are lame and hefty people who are way funnier, smarter, and cooler. But some people forget and go overboard trying to achieve the ideal body that they are sure will solve all their problems. They tend to become obsessed with their weight and totally focused on being thin, like that's the best way to be and anything less is ugly. It's a warped way of looking at life and is completely unhealthy, but it happens all the time.

Lots of teens struggle with eating disorders by either starving themselves (anorexia), bingeing and purging (bulimia), or eating and then exercising to the point of exhaustion. Some image-obsessed teens even use body-building steroids as a shortcut to bulking up. They don't realize that they are hurting their bodies and their minds. The only way to lose weight and keep it off while remaining healthy is to eat a balanced diet and exercise regularly and reasonably. When your body feels strong and fit, your skin glows, your eyes sparkle, and you radiate from the inside out. And that is beautiful!

Pressure Cooker

Ten percent of high school students suffer from some type of eating disorder. If you notice one of your pals doing damage to her body, get help fast! Your friend might fight you on it now, but she'll be grateful in the long run.

Height is another physical trait that we would love to have control over. Are you the type of person who has heard "How's the weather up there?" one too many times? Or do you wish people said that to you? If you are very short or very tall, you are sure to stand out in the crowd when all you ever really want is to blend in. The 6-foot girl and the 5-foot guy have it the roughest. Their bodies defy the norms, and they often find themselves over-compensating. She may slouch low in her seat while he wants to stand high on a chair, both trying to even out the stakes.

Besides height and weight, you're also changing in other ways. You are on your way to becoming a man or a woman, but you aren't quite there yet. Although you may still feel like a kid, your body might tell a different story. Sometimes, the reverse is true. You consider yourself an adult—you just wish your body would hurry and catch up!

As you get older and become more body-conscious, you can't help but check out your classmates and their progress in the great maturity race. You must have noticed the chest on the girl who sits next to you in English. Her body says "Va-va-va-voom" while yours barely makes a peep. And you know that dude who sits behind you? Where'd he get those bulging muscles? That is so not fair! You and he were always the same size until about a year ago. And then, bam! He's like some kind of beefy hunk and you feel, well, left in his dust. No matter how many times you hear that everyone matures at a different rate, it doesn't make you feel any better when some of your peers have the bodies of 20-year-olds and you look like you still need a babysitter.

Consider those other teens, the ones whose bodies have grown way faster. Maybe you are one yourself. That's no cake walk, either. Think about it—how strange to watch your body suddenly turn into something that looks more like it belongs to a teacher than a student. People start noticing, and suddenly you're getting some attention that's very different than anything you've experienced before. That's no fun. Just try being the first in your class to have to wear a bra and getting it snapped by the obnoxious boys who think they're being funny. Or, consider the guy who suddenly has a mustache, not full-on thick like your uncle the cop, just a little fuzzy thing that looks like he's been eating crayons. Total bummer.

The truth of the matter is that nobody is completely happy with their body. We all curse Mom and Dad for those "bad" genes we inherited. But, remember, sometimes what seems so bad isn't really that awful; it's just different than what you wish you looked like. Next time you want to walk out of your house wearing a paper bag over your head, remember, chances are good that no one else notices the things about your body that bug you so much. Or, maybe they do and they think they're awesome.

Kids with a Clue

"I was ten years old when I bought my first bra. All of my friends were still wearing undershirts, and when I had to change for gym, I hated every second of it."

—Stephanie, age 15

As difficult as it is to make your body look the way you want it to, your hair is a lot easier to control. Of course, we're all born with different hair types, colors, and thickness. But there is a lot you can do to take charge of it.

People constantly pull and tug at their hair. They bleach it, tint it, dye it, iron it, curl it, relax it, add weaves, add streaks, add highlights—all in an attempt to get *that* look. We've all wanted that look—the hip, in, and happening look that you like, want, and need to have. People spend millions of dollars a year on their hair, and teens make up a big chunk of that change. Where once girls were the only ones working on their locks, guys are now quickly following suit. They, too, are realizing the joys of bleaching, dying, and other general fussing. Changing your hair is an easy way to revamp your look and make you feel like part of the gang.

My Cell Phone's Smaller Than Your Cell Phone

Face it: You're a teenager, and you want it all. You probably feel entitled to it. It always seems like everybody has everything and that you're the one who looks like a deprived loser. There is nothing worse in the whole world than when your parents have the nerve to tell you "No." How could they claim to love you and in the same breath deny you the one thing, the only thing (at least for today) that you desperately want?

Acquiring status symbols becomes more important in your teens than ever before. There is no question that all of us would love to be the proud owners of the most expensive, the most luxurious, the most incredible ... anything. But as important as having that thing may seem at the moment, owning it won't make the clouds part and the sun shine down.

Vice Advice

Stop moping about what you don't have and appreciate what your parents do give you. A little gratitude goes a long way. Maybe if you thank them for the CD instead of whining that you wanted the box set, they might shock you next time and scrape together some extra dough to buy you concert tickets.

Not all of you spend your time dreaming of the stuff you want and can't have. Some of you are fortunate enough to have everything. Your parents can afford to buy you the best of the best, and they do. But do you appreciate it? Make sure that you're aware that the things you might take for granted are probably coveted by some of your classmates.

Often, you see a beautiful pop star walk down the red carpet at the MTV Awards in a dress that costs more than your entire closet put together. The first question reporters ask is always "*Who* are you wearing?" Never is the answer the name of the bargain basement store where you bought your prom dress. Why is it that the world is so obsessed with name brands?

Is there really such a difference between jeans costing $60 and ones that look almost identical selling for $360? Yes, there is—the expensive pair is usually made from better materials and meant to last longer. But before running out and investing a hard earned month's salary from the yogurt shop on the fancy pants, think logically. What makes those expensive jeans so spectacular anyway? You might absolutely love the Italian leather hip-huggers, but the pair made in Ohio looks pretty much the same and is just as cool. So think twice before you crack open your piggy bank.

Designer logos are a neon sign to the world that you shelled out the big bucks to wear a name brand. You know the clothes, the ones with a giant emblem in the center, proudly announcing how much you spent on them. You pay a ton of money just for the trademark, but if all your friends strut around in one, you're going to want to also. And unlike the zebra shoes, a knock-off just won't cut it; it's the real deal or nothing at all. If you absolutely must emblazon the company name across your chest, do it. But, remember, they aren't paying you to model or to advertise—you're paying them. Limit the number in your wardrobe and keep the money in your own pocket.

You probably have other ideas on how to spend that cash anyway. For instance, you are never too old for toys. The plastic walkie-talkies that you owned as a kid are replaced by the high-tech gadgets that nobody can live without. And, just like when you were seven, whoever has the best toys wins. This can become quite an expensive competition: Electronic address books cost a heck of a lot more than the paper kind with the gold letters and the rainbow cover. And forget about walking down the hallway without hearing somebody's pager go off or the musical chirping of a cell phone ring. Those days are over.

If you don't own all the electronic essentials, you feel totally out of the techno loop. With all of your friends in constant communication 24/7, you can't keep up with just the rotary-dial dinosaur that your dad calls a classic. You need these modern accessories now, the way you needed that pogo stick then.

Don't freak out over being the only one on the block without an e-mail pager. There was a time, not long ago, when teenagers didn't even have phones in their rooms, let alone a private line, an Internet dial-up, and a cell phone small enough to fit in a back pocket. This may sound archaic, but it really wasn't so bad. Nowadays, anybody can find you at any time of the day, regardless of whether it's convenient for you. Not owning these toys is not necessarily a bad thing. Granted, you don't know the details the minute the action happens, but stories get better with each telling—by the time you hear the news, it is probably even juicier. So, if you are one of the many without the technology of the moment, don't be bummed. Cherish your inaccessibility and consider your time more valuable.

The thing you probably consider more valuable than your time is your car. It doesn't matter who you are, what you like, or where you're going—everybody wants to arrive in style. What you drive makes a definite statement to the public. In some schools, you are a nobody if you don't have a brand new fully-loaded German import. In others, the only ride to be seen in is an old-school classic American hot rod with a sweet chrome finish and fuzzy dice. Even if you prefer the low rider pick-up with the expensive stereo system, the biggest and most powerful SUV on the market, or some other fancy automobile, one fact overrides everything: You have waited a lifetime to get your license, and there is nothing like the freedom of the open road. Whether you're cruising on hot wheels or driving your little sister's carpool in Mom's clunky mini van with the headlight held on by duct tape, you're still in the driver's seat, and that is cooler than anything.

Of course, the world would be a way better place if we all got to own the cars that we really wanted—or any car at all. But, come on, life isn't that perfect. Unfortunately, even if you dream about what a rock star you would be cruising down the road in a sweet convertible with all the girls yelling your name as you drive by, sometimes there's no way you can afford the killer car. If you're one of the carless millions who feels like a big loser as he sadly drags himself onto the school bus each morning, keep your chin up. It's only a matter of time before you have your own set of wheels. Meanwhile, bum rides from your friends and chip in for gas. It's still better than hoofing it.

Following Fads

If you've ever seen a teen movie from the 1980s, you know that big hair was everywhere. People wore fluorescent ties, splatter-painted sweatshirts, and fingerless lace gloves—sometimes all at once. Ugh!

The fashion police must have had the decade off. Even though these things were the epitome of cool then, they are seriously dorky today. Such is the trap that you fall into when you are a slave to a fad.

Fads are a bizarre phenomenon. There's no telling what will catch on and what will never get off the ground. Some are started by celebrities, some in foreign countries, and some on the city streets right around the corner. Regardless of where they come from, these fast and furious styles can wrap you up and take you for a ride whether you like it or not. When a fad catches on, you might feel forced to jump on the bandwagon without knowing why. If all the popular kids at school start wearing a particular kind of jeans or a type of barrette in their hair, should you? You might not like how it looks, or you might not even consider your own taste. You just know that you *have* to wear it if you want to be like everyone else.

A fad is a temporary, usually irrational, movement adopted because of its prestige. There are two words in this definition to pay special attention to: *temporary* and *irrational.* Some fads last a while—a short while, but a while nonetheless. Most are over before you can say "Beanie Babies."

For years, fads have been responsible for sending herds of people to the mall desperate to own that elusive whatever so that they can be up to the minute and not look out of touch. Your parents went through it, and their parents went through it. But how many of these old fads would send you scurrying to the store today?

- Leg warmers
- Hula hoops
- Fingerless lace gloves
- Pet rocks
- Smiley face buttons
- Sea monkeys

Probably not many. Most fads seem downright silly in retrospect and are gone in the blink of an eye, easily forgotten. Some fads are harmless even though many are potentially expensive. Clothes come and go and only take up room in your closet. And haircuts will grow out eventually although you might need to wear a hat for a while. Other fads, however, aren't as easy to get over. Tattoos and body piercing are permanent physical alterations, so be careful and think long and hard before you get ink or metal. It's a decision that you'll wear forever.

Kids with a Clue

"Jasmine and I had been together for two years, and we talked about getting married after graduation. I surprised her by getting her name tattooed on my arm. Well, we broke up a month later, and now I'm stuck with it. How am I going to find another girl named Jasmine?"

—Billy, age 17

What You See Isn't Always What You Get

Doesn't it bug you when people at school take one look at you and think they know your life story? How could they possibly comprehend the depths of your soul based on the sneakers you are wearing? They can't, but they do. And much as you might hate to admit it, you do the exact same thing. That boy with the long black hair, the leather jacket, and the eye liner is definitely a screw-up, and the girl with the long blond curls, the tight sweater, and the high-pitched voice is a bimbo who sleeps around. Right?

Wrong. The guy reads computer magazines and volunteers at a homeless shelter. And the girl is ranked first in your class and has never been kissed. Looks are definitely deceiving, and the jury has already come in on these two with a guilty verdict. Now imagine what they say about you. Frightening, isn't it?

Kids with a Clue

"I'm totally shy, and when I started my new school, I barely talked to anybody. People just automatically thought that I was mean and stuck-up. It was the worst. That is so not me."

—Mandy, age 14

Take a long, hard look at your friends. Study them closely. Who do they remind you of? Each other? You? Most likely. But that's no surprise. You're probably friends in the first place because you have similar taste and are into a lot of the same stuff. You guys also dress similarly and have a certain collective look.

Some cliques dress in a very specific way. Your interests often play a large part in dictating your style. If you're into sports, there is probably a pretty specific way the athletes in your school dress. If you're the type who cannot wait to audition for the school play, you may coordinate with the students who are into acting and theater.

The music that you listen to often influences your outer appearance as well. Had we known in the 1990s that grunge would change the lives of millions of listeners, we definitely would have bought stock in flannel shirts. Fashion has felt the influence of music for decades. Check out the photos of teens in the 1960s. Like the nerdy bowl haircuts on both guys and girls? "Moptops" were all the rage thanks to four lads from Liverpool. They were in a small band you might have heard of, called the Beatles. They were the cool group, and they determined the cool style. Sound crazy? But is it really different now?

It may seem boring to you that the misery chick's wardrobe ranges from black to dark black, but she'd rather yank out her eyebrow ring with pliers than wear your good-luck basketball jersey. But it makes sense when you realize that she is into goth music and you turn on the radio only to hear the game. Before you write her off as some freak you would never give the time of day to, consider this: You may change your clothes and your interests, but you'll always be you. Ten years from now, that goth might be a conservative Wall-Street trader with season tickets to the theater, and you might be a blue-haired club promoter of techno raves. You never know. Chances are, you two are probably not as different as the ways you dress.

Here is an experiment for you to try tomorrow at school:

1. Find someone you don't know who has a style totally different from your own.

2. Get over your anxiety, don't worry about what your friends will think, and introduce yourself.

3. Start small-talking and find out what movies that person likes, who his favorite band is, or what classes she hates.

4. Be pleasantly surprised when you realize that underneath, this person is a lot like you.

This may sound unlikely, but it's not. No matter what they look like, other teens are going through the exact same growing pains you are, and nobody has an easy time of it. You may choose to lose yourself in heavy metal music or let your hair dread while the guy next to you pumps more iron than a professional wrestler or neatly presses his blue jeans. But all of you are insecure about one thing or another, and everybody just wants to be liked. So, the next time you jump to conclusions about someone that you don't really know, take a second to remember your new friend from the hallway. That hippie chick might despise history just as much as you do.

Now what about how adults see you? Do your parents like your friends? Some pals your mom practically wants to adopt while others rub her the wrong way and are never invited to stay for dinner. Parents are only human, and they often make assumptions about your buddies. Some they see as good influences, and others they think are monsters who will corrupt their little angel. They see a "young man" all neat and tucked in who says "please" and "thank you" and automatically think that he can teach you a thing or two.

Well, if Mom knew that sweet little Johnny was the biggest pothead on campus, she might be singing a different tune.

And what about that quiet girl who can't make eye contact with adults and leaves without saying good-bye to your parents? They don't trust her a bit. They are sure she's shifty and sneaky, definitely responsible for the C minus you're getting in biology. Wouldn't they be stunned to know that without her help, that C minus would be an F?

Your teachers, the principal, and the guy who owns the pizza joint are just as guilty of snap judgments. They will take one look at you and decide whether you are going to make their lives easier or whether they have to watch your every move like a hawk. Even though clean-cut boys can instigate a fight, it's the muscle-bound tough guy who's going to be accused of starting it.

First impressions are not necessarily accurate ones. We all want people to acknowledge who we are on the inside, but the truth is, it's very hard to get past the outside. The best way to conquer this is to make that change yourself and look beneath the surface to find the real deal. Hopefully, others will follow your lead.

The Least You Need to Know

- All body types are beautiful in their own way, so appreciate yours.

- Don't define yourself by what you own. You're more valuable than anything you can buy.

- Be wary of the latest craze. It could come and go faster than your crush-of-the-moment.

- What you see isn't always what you get, so don't make snap judgments about your peers.

Chapter 4

High School Hierarchy

In This Chapter

- Holding the hot ticket to cool
- Different strokes for different folks
- Blurring the clique lines
- Flying solo through school skies

There is a comfort to knowing the place where you belong. During the tumultuous teen years, everyone is searching furiously for that place. You're looking for someone to sit with at lunch, to walk home with after volleyball practice, and hopefully, to share some laughs with along this rocky road of teenage-hood. We all gravitate naturally toward people who are similar to us. But what does this mean in the grand scheme of the social structure of school? In this chapter, we'll discuss the advantages and disadvantages of belonging to a clique, and we'll try to make sense of the constant crazy quest for popularity.

Membership Has Its Privileges

The politics of the high school hallways can be just as intricate and juicy as those inside the White House. The teenage social rat race is an interesting phenomenon, partially because it is a world without rules. It's lawless and anarchic, like the Old West, but with baseball hats instead of ten-gallons. Biting and scratching are not only allowed, but encouraged. The possibilities are endless, and anything can happen.

Although there are similarities and themes that go across the board, no two schools are alike. Some schools are so socially rigid that the fate of one's popularity may rest solely in the hands of a few golden Princes and Princesses of Popularity. It may not be fair, but it happens all the time. In many hallowed halls of learning, cliques and the ladder of popularity are extremely clear and structured. You know where you fit in and so does everyone else. Peer group boundaries are solid and as difficult to budge as a sumo wrestler. If you're a brain, you hang out with the brains and that's it. There are very few instances of "social mobility" within the ranks.

In a school only a few miles away, the attitudes may be more laid-back and the clique lines more relaxed and free-flowing. Some schools do not have much of a social structure at all. Teens separate into groups naturally, but they may just be considered different rather than better or worse, popular or unpopular. Extremely large schools are often more lax purely because of the immense size of the student body.

The desire to be a member of a peer group is completely normal and incredibly powerful at this age. Being part of one is not necessary, but it can be a valuable experience. It makes you feel like you belong somewhere, which is a welcome comfort in a world that can be stressful, scary, and lonely. There is a strong need for this sense of belonging during adolescence when you're often reeling. You're confused and insecure about how you're supposed to look and behave.

When surrounded by others your age, you have something to compare yourself to. This can be both a blessing and a curse. The looks and actions of a group will define what's considered "normal" in thought, behavior, and body. It can be a wonderful guide and comfort, especially when you're constantly feeling out of it. However, too much comparing is a bad thing and can be dangerous, providing you with a very skewed image of what is normal.

Pressure Cooker

Some teens become so obsessed with comparing themselves to their peers that they wind up with an unhealthy self-image and extremely low self-esteem.

Inclusion in a social group also gives you an identity apart from your family. Relationships with your friends become more important every day. Trouble with your compadres can seem life-shattering and can totally throw you for a loop. The bonds that you have formed with them have become almost familial. To an extent, they have taken the place of your relationships with your blood relatives. You still love your family, but even breathing around them has become a chore. Plain and simple, they drive you nuts. You want them to understand you and to see you for who you are, but they just don't. You've begun to feel alienated from them, but, thank goodness, your friends have stepped up to the plate. They get it—they get everything because they're going through the same growing pains.

Everyone naturally gravitates toward people they have stuff in common with. Teens are no different. You're on a quest to find that elusive group of peers that provides you the perfect match, a team of players that fit you like a glove. You are looking for others who are like you—at least, in some of the important ways. You want to be around people with the same interests, likes, and dislikes that you have. They remind you that you're normal and that your "thing" is not only accepted, but a-okay. Besides that, it's just nice to have people to talk to about the stuff that makes you tick. It's a pleasant surprise to find pals who have also been counting the days until tickets to that reggae festival go on sale, just like you have been, mon. It's way more fun to hang out with someone who's just as into decorating for the prom as you are than with the kid who's boycotting because he thinks that organized activities are bogus.

Some peer groups are just like packs of wolves. They do everything together—hang out in the halls, eat lunch, join the same teams and clubs, party on the weekends. Being one of them is a full-time job—just don't expect a paycheck. While being a wolf has its advantages, like always having companions around, it can sometimes feel like system overload. You may be so much a part of the group that it seems like you don't even count as your own person. Your identity as one of the pack totally overshadows your own personality and individuality.

Many cliques have lots of rules and constraints even though they may be subtle or unspoken. You have to stay on your toes to make sure you are living within the boundaries. Deviating from the norm may be extremely discouraged and can even be detrimental to your position in the group. You may even feel like you can't truly be yourself.

Kids with a Clue

"With my group of friends at school, every day is a fashion show. You have to wear the best clothes and always look done up. If I came in one day wearing sweats with my hair in a ponytail, they would totally drop me."

—Kara, age 17

The pressure to conform to a group is strong and sometimes seems worth it since membership has its privileges. There may be a specific group you have your eye on, and being a part of it means something special to you. Maybe you really like one of the members, either platonically or romantically. What better way to get yourself closer to the prize than to be part of that person's crowd?

The cool image of a group can be as enticing as an overpriced ice cream cone at an amusement park in July. Being one of them can offer you opportunities and open doors to stuff that you couldn't otherwise access. If you want to bond with the cheerleaders, being on the football team will probably get you invited to their parties. That's kind of a sweet deal just for hanging with the right people. Getting your body pounded at practice six times a week might seem a small price to pay for that ticket in.

The Popularity Circus

The desire to achieve popularity is strange and powerful. Some people will go to great lengths in an attempt to be a part of a certain clique or to be considered one of the elite. It's a dirty business, the popularity gig. And it makes otherwise nice, normal teenagers do weird, crazy things.

Being popular means different things in different schools. The importance of popularity varies as does the way it is defined. Some common denominators are pretty obvious. Unfortunately, superficiality and shallowness play a big role here. Good-looking people tend to be admired because they are romantically desirable. Fortunately, people are also attracted to strength and confidence. These traits are the reason why some teens become natural leaders that others willingly follow.

Just as high schools vary, so do the separations of cliques, groups, and crowds. During the teen years, just as you are figuring out what you're into, so is everyone else. Hopefully along the way, you will cross paths with others you have things in common with. Similar interests will likely attract you to a group as will its image and reputation. If the school reveres it as cool and popular, you want in.

Some teens are always playing the piano for the school recital, volunteering to act out scenes in drama class, or drawing cartoons for the school newspaper. They are the creative types, and they treasure every minute that they can exercise their passion. Whether they are in the marching band, a head-banging garage band, or are just really into the hottest boy band, they need to satisfy their craving for tunes. Maybe they love to read poetry or write their own comic books. They might paint, sculpt, or draw on cafeteria napkins. Strong creative impulses drive this type to want to surround themselves with others who feel the same artistic draw.

Other teens are more of the bookish type. School can be a bummer sometimes, but for them, it's never because of their classes. Everyone has a favorite subject, but theirs gets them out of bed in the morning. These are the kids who hand in their papers early and whose physics projects always win the Science Fair. They may have already figured out that they want to be engineers or biologists, thanks to some enthusiastic teachers and amazing classes they've taken. They are academic enthusiasts—and proud of it.

And what about the students who'd rather run around a field, a track, or a court than after the cute girl or guy in their homeroom? They are athletic aces all the way. These die-hard team players love everything about being an athlete and cheering on others. Whether it's watching a pro game on TV or supporting the local peewee tee-ball tykes, they are happiest around sports.

Some teens are social butterflies at birth. They pop out of the womb chit-chatting with all the other babies in the nursery. They grow up loving being in the middle of the action, surrounded by friends and conversation and giggling. These flutterers do have other interests, sure, but they feel most at home outside the house and live for hanging with their amigos.

Similar types of cliques exist at every school although they have varying reputations. Different groups are considered cool depending on where you go. There are several reasons for this. Sometimes, coolness is based on the group's individual members. After all, if Lovely Rita hangs with that group of monkeys, they've got to be cool monkeys. Because everyone worships Rita, she's got to know what's down, right?

Sometimes, a group develops a heavenly reputation because they are part of a strong school program. If your school's debate team has been state champs every year for the last decade, the team is probably considered the "in" exclusive group. In this school, the brains rule what's cool. And if your field hockey team makes it to the nationals almost every year, the girls with the sticks win at the popularity polls.

The opposite is true as well. Some groups at school may have a negative connotation. They may be perceived as nerdy or uncool even though those labels were probably placed on them totally unfairly. You may have an interest that you squelch only because you don't want to be affiliated with a group that has a geeky reputation. Maybe the marching band in your school is thought of as unhip. Or perhaps the drama club is considered an artsy fartsy bunch. You may love to act or can really make the sax sing, but now something is holding you back, and it's not you. It's what you fear people will think of you if you join.

Vice Advice

If you really love something, then do it. Don't let an uncool stereotype stop you from following your passion. Maybe your joining can change the status from geek to great.

Then, there are the ones who don't fit into any of the major groups or cliques at school. Although you may not realize it, there are a lot of these teens—maybe even you. You're really not into any of the stuff that makes up these other factions. You have no idea how people can be so into hitting a little ball with a stick and then running around some crazy diamond. It seems so pointless. And your classes are okay, but you don't exactly get all goosebumpy when someone utters the words "Bunsen burner." You probably think that this wacky social structure is kind of ridiculous, but you're still wondering where you fit in and, more importantly, whether you have to.

Well, heck, ladies and gents, you certainly don't need to be worrying your little heads about that. You are your own person, doing your own thing. And you're sure not alone. You don't have to live a high-profile high school life to have a good time. You just have to do the things you want to do regardless of what you think you're supposed to be doing. Chances are, your high school experience isn't much different from the people in those other cliques, anyway. In fact, it might be even better because you don't have the added stress of conformity.

You can enjoy school, have good friends, and lead a sweet extra-curricular life no matter where you find yourself in the solar system of school. Just stay in control and be the person you want to be. No social status, popular or not, can or should change who you are inside.

That might be all well and good, but you may still be unhappy with your mediocre status. You crave popularity. You want it so badly that you're willing to sell your firstborn to gain entry through those glittery gates. Despite how important your standing at school may feel to you, being popular is not the answer to all of life's questions. Just ask one of the school royalty, and they'll tell you that it's not the golden ticket. Popular kids have problems, insecurities, and shortcomings just like you.

Kids with a Clue

"I used to want to be friends with this one group of guys so bad. They are the bosses of our school, and everyone worships them. But, once I got into their group, I realized they were bullying jerks. I was better off before."

—Billy, age 17

And think for a second about what makes these kids cool, anyway. Are they really that smart or that funny or that good-looking? Sometimes when you take a step back, you can't see much that's cool at all. They may be bullies, put on a pedestal because people are just too scared to stand up to them.

Now, what if you are popular, or a member of the cool circle at your school? Of course, there's nothing wrong with that, either. If you're happy with this high-profile job and content with your friends, then you're probably in the right place for you. But your popularity is not your "Get out of jail free" card. Be careful not to buy too much into the hype, and don't take one of those nasty power trips. Your membership to that group does not entitle you to be a brat. Obnoxious, mean, or pretentious behavior is inexcusable in any circumstance. Your group may have a certain level of power at school, which is not to be abused. Being a part of any group should not define who you are or how good a person you are. As a part of your clique, you are not automatically better than anyone else. But you can try to be, by being kind and good to people, no matter how the others in your group behave.

The easiest way to find your own niche is to just be yourself. No one knows what's best for you but you. Remember, being popular means that people like you, and there are lots of ways to achieve that. Start by reaching out to others. If you are a nice person and go out of your way to be friendly, you'll have fans who will sing your praises no matter what you look like, who else you're friends with, or what group you do or don't belong to. By going out on a limb and being a good friend, you will become popular to individuals regardless of what your school social structure is like. That's a way cooler way to be because it's real and it's personal and has nothing to do with the shallowness that we've all been caught up in at one time or another.

Not Always Status Quo

Jocks, cheerleaders, skaters, brainiacs, punks, goths, nerds. It takes all kinds to make up an interesting and colorful student body. These groups are all valuable additions to the diversity of your hallways. They each contribute something totally different. But nobody wants to always hang with the same types of people. Being around a bunch of "yous" all the time can be suffocating. We're all way more complicated than that.

Variation keeps life interesting. No matter how good something is or how much you like it, too much of the same old thing gets boring. Even if fried peanut-butter-and-banana sandwiches are your favorite food, you'd never want to eat them for breakfast, lunch, and dinner every day. Eventually, this culinary classic would totally gross you out. Overdosing on the same people has the same effect. It takes many different types to keep your taste buds happy.

Hanging out with the same bunch day in and day out is bound to get stale sooner or later. A good remedy for this is to give other people a chance. Ever have a class that you were sure you would absolutely loathe? Then, you sat through a couple of days and realized that it was not as bad as you thought, and actually it was kind of interesting. All of a sudden an entire world that you didn't even know existed was opened up to you. And to think that you almost wrote it off completely. There are probably people at school who you have disregarded just like that class. It's a foolish move. You may be shutting yourself off from someone who could be the next great addition to your life.

It's a cool thing to be friends with all types of people. It feels great to walk down the hall at school and have tons of different kinds of teens from a million different cliques to say "howdy" to. Your social life is about more than just who to party with. It can expose you to new things and broaden your horizons. Good friendships are satisfying, especially with people who add something to your life. Cultivating an eclectic group of friends is a great way to expand your world. People with different interests can teach each other about what rocks their world. Maybe, you never thought about mountain biking before, but your new friend Freddy, who is on a racing team and everything, invited you along. Now, you're saving your pennies to buy your own dirt devil.

Rigid clique boundaries make it easy to forget that there's a world outside your immediate circle of friends. Fight the tendency to exist in a social bubble. Open your eyes, open your mind, and cross-clique. Your life will be fuller and guaranteed more exciting.

The One-Man Show

Plenty of teens are not part of groups or cliques or teams or even many friendships. They are living their lives outside the tangled web of the mainstream social world of their schools. Maybe you're one of these teens doing you own thing. Whether it's by choice or not, you find yourself separated from the rest of your peers.

No one wants to feel alone, and everyone needs good friends. Maybe, you are having a hard time finding others who are interested in the same things you are. This may make you feel awkward and out of place. You want to fit in, but no matter what you do, you just don't—at least, not the way you want to. Even if you buy the "right" clothes or try to act the "cool" way, you still don't blend. But there is a great value to being your own person and living your life outside the chaos of the social world of your school. It can actually be way cooler if you give it a chance.

Kids with a Clue

"I always felt like an alien at school. All the other kids were so cookie cutter and I just couldn't fit in. Well, I gave up trying and just did my own thing. Now they are all wanting to be friends with me."

—Maya, age 14

Going solo in school is not an easy thing in a land that seems to be dominated by groups. It's definitely a heck of a lot easier to go along with the crowd. After all, there is safety in numbers and all that jazz. Plus, it's easier to just go with the flow and let yourself get swept up in that pack mentality where others dictate how you dress, how you look, and how you behave. There's no real reason to worry about yourself as a person since the group identity is similar enough to your own.

You know those students at school, the ones who always seem to be in their own solar system. Maybe, they dress a little strangely or listen to weird music. Even though they march to the beat of their own drum, there's something about them that you really dig. Their individuality is admirable. These trendsetters have the guts to dress the way they want and act the way they please even if it's different from everyone else.

Learn to embrace your individuality. Learn to love what makes you different. The power of the individual is strong and has limitless potential. Deciding to do your own thing rather than trying to always fit into someone else's mold gives you complete freedom. Living life the way you want to and at your own pace means never having to slow down for anyone. You're completely at your own mercy, for a change, and no one else's. The goal is to be an originator, not an imitator.

It takes guts to go against the grain and walk alone when surrounded by this extreme pressure to fit in. But if you can do it, if you have the strength to say "Phooey!" to the cliquey world around you, standing on your own and enjoying it can be a way more satisfying reward.

The Least You Need to Know

- Being a member of a certain group or clique does have its privileges. But be aware of the price you must pay to belong, and decide whether it is worth it for you.

- Before you throw yourself into trying to achieve popularity, stop and consider why you want it so badly. You may be bowing down to pressure put on you by people you don't even like or respect.

- It's no fun to be categorized all the time. Your life will be richer if you are friends with people because of who they are, not who they hang out with.

- Groups, shmoops. If you're not into being a part of a clique, back off and do your own thing. Being your own person means freedom, control, and the power to act the way you want to, not the way you're expected to.

Part **3**

The Challenge to Act Cool

Everybody wants to be cool. We all strive to be "it" in one way or another. While sometimes this goal pushes you to try harder to be more successful, at other times it can lead you down the path to destruction.

The next few chapters get down and dirty with the bad behaviors some teens take on to be part of the crowd. Some are hurtful to your peers, such as teasing and name-calling. Others are flat-out disrespectful whether to your folks or to your teachers. Then there's the whole sex issue, which isn't always done for the right reasons. And we can't forget drugs and alcohol, for which there are no right reasons. Chances are, you know a little something about a lot of these actions, but read on to learn about their repercussions.

Chapter 5

Do Unto Others

In This Chapter

- Sticks and stones may break my bones
- Running through the rumor mill
- If I wanted you to know, I would have said it so you could hear me
- Feeling left out in the cold
- When the tables suddenly turn
- Which side of the peer-pressure fence are you on?

At a young age, you were taught to treat other people the way you want to be treated. It sounds like a very simple concept and one that should be easy to adhere to. However, day in and day out, people show each other an amazing lack of respect. What is this utter disregard about, and why does it happen? In this chapter, we examine the different ways teens attack one another with bad behavior.

Teasing

As soon as you knew how to talk, you knew how to tease. There wasn't a day that went by in nursery school when someone didn't stick out his tongue and chant the familiar "Nah nah nah nah nah. I have a 'fill-in-the-blank' and you don't." Being on the receiving end of one of these sessions was almost as embarrassing as getting scolded by Mommy in front of the other kids. Even then you wanted to be cool, and that was so not it.

As you got older, the teasing got more descriptive and you entered into the world of name-calling. This form of harassment is one of the most blatant types of peer pressure. Teens use mean terms to label each other in order to make their prey feel bad about themselves. If you are afraid to do something, you are instantly called a chicken. It doesn't matter if the focus of your fear is dangerous, like jumping out of a plane, or could get you into trouble, like stealing a car; the slightest showing of weakness is all it takes to get teased.

Even character traits that are seemingly normal, if not admirable, could be enough to attract name-callers. If you are smart and do well in school, you've probably been called a "nerd" at some point. If you play football, invariably you've heard the term "dumb jock" before. Date a few guys, and before you know it, someone calls you "easy." The truth is you could be smart and the coolest kid in town, the quarterback with perfect SAT scores, or outgoing yet prudish, and it won't matter a bit. Name-calling doesn't have to be truthful; it just has to hurt.

Teens love to obnoxiously point out when someone is different from the group. The dissimilarity might be something that you are able to dictate, like whether you shave your head or have a nose ring. Sometimes, however, attacks extend to characteristics that are beyond your control. If you are teased about your height and have earned nicknames like Munchkin or Stretch, your options are limited. Sure, you could wear platforms or walk on your knees, but you won't fool anyone. You're stuck being harassed. And it sucks.

Often, there is absolutely no logic at all behind the name-calling. Someone wants to make fun of you, so they call you a geek. Well, you've never done anything geeky—in fact, you have always been pretty cool. But now, this label is floating around your head, and it is driving you crazy. Your self-confidence is shaken, and you wrack your brain trying to figure out why in the world anybody would possibly call you that. You begin to scrutinize your every move. Could you indeed be a geek and not even know it?! The horror!

Kids with a Clue

"I have these two really pointy teeth and everybody calls me 'vampire.' I hate it, but there's nothing I can do to change my teeth. I just wish everyone would forget about them and move on."

—Joey, age 14

You have just fallen victim to an obvious peer-pressure ploy. The name-caller is probably somebody you don't even like, yet here you are becoming obsessed with that person's opinion. He wanted to get under your skin, and he did—all because you let him. It's not easy to ignore teasing, but it is important to consider the source. Your real friends would never set out to intentionally hurt your feelings, and they are the ones whose opinions matter most.

Sometimes, teasing takes another form, putting others down. Cutting remarks like these are a low blow that bitingly critiques a specific behavior. The most common put-down is calling somebody "stupid" because they don't know something that the offender considers common knowledge. You could be a rocket scientist who does brain surgery on the weekends, but if you don't know which teams are in the Final Four, the jocko next to you who watches sports all day long will call you an idiot. As moronic as this is, getting into it with the gorilla in the next seat would be a waste of your time.

Attacks on intelligence are not the only ones that sting. People make fun of everything: clothes, hair, car, you name it. These dirty digs can hurt—badly. You may absolutely love the new sneakers that your mom just bought you, but if someone at school makes fun of their color or says that they're cheap, you suddenly want to kick them off your feet and bury them in the bottom of your closet with the bunny-rabbit pajamas from Grandma.

Some cruel words don't insult one victim; they condemn an entire culture. Racism, religious prejudice, and intolerance are extreme forms of put-downs. What cheap shots! Any type of tease or cutting remark makes the attacker look more like a loser than the victim. These particular jabs show that the offender is a small-minded, bigoted fool who should not only be disregarded, but quickly taught a lesson. These prejudiced simpletons are in dire need of a tolerance class to show them there is more to life than what is in their uneducated heads.

Have You Heard ...

Few things in life are worse than being the subject of a vicious rumor. You walk into school one morning and can sense instantly that something is off. Your casual buddies seem too busy to say hello to you. Rather than jumping to conclusions, you cut them some slack and figure that their snubbing you is more about the big chem test everyone's stressing over. You continue on to your locker, where you spot that hottie you've been crushing. You are shocked when you are not only ignored, but shot a dirty look as well. Now, you are convinced something is up. You look around and notice that beady eyes are staring at you from behind their textbooks. Ill at ease, you're trying to bury your head in your locker when your best friend approaches, grabs your arm, and pulls you into the bathroom for an emergency chat. You are shocked to find out that apparently the whole school thinks that you are a narc working undercover for the cops and are going to bust them all. How untrue can you get? You're so not in cahoots. You don't even like to watch cop shows!

Rumors get started quickly and easily. All it takes is a few whispered words to change a person's reputation. Gossip spreads like wildfire, but it starts with only two little sticks igniting. Before you know it, the entire place is ablaze with scandal. Most of the time, the rumors aren't even true and are started completely innocently. Wires were crossed, and someone got an idea in her head and passed it on to a friend, who told another friend, who added a few of his own embellishments. This is very similar to the children's game "telephone." The whispered sentence "Mary went to the store to buy bread with Johnny" can end up as "Mary wants to score in bed with Johnny." Now, poor Mary is given weird looks and is being thought of as a slut, all because somebody told someone else that she went food shopping with her friend Johnny.

Pressure Cooker

A nasty rumor could destroy self-confidence, and innocent teens may feel overwhelmed by their bad reputations. Rather than fighting, they find it easier to just live up to them.

Sometimes, gossip is started as revenge. You might have done something to another teen, either voluntarily or accidentally, that she is not thrilled about. She seeks vengeance, and the quickest way to get that is by spreading a nasty rumor. Even if it is a total fabrication, the effect is still powerful. There is now a story floating around your school that is unflattering, to say the least, and detrimental to your reputation.

Examples of gossip in its extreme form are found in tabloid newspapers. You know the ones, with the flashy headlines that you sneak a peak at in the checkout line at the grocery store. They are responsible for breaking stories like "Alien Builds Colony in Old Woman's Backyard" or "Woman Gives Birth to Fifty-Year-Old Man." While these articles amuse us momentarily, they pass quickly out of our minds. However, the tabloids run other stories that are much more damaging. Celebrity gossip that appears in these rags can wreck families, damage careers, and destroy egos, all for the sole purpose of making money. If the current "it" girl graces the cover, people are going to buy it. The story inside has an exclusive scoop from her mother's brother's trainer's best friend that she's on a dog food diet. While this is obviously a lie that nobody is going to take seriously, the young starlet is now teased about sharing a bowl with Fido.

Things are no different in your school. If there is a rumor that you messed around with your best friend's significant other, you are going to be thought of as a home wrecker. You may never have been alone together, but the gossip is circulating and the seeds of doubt have been planted about you. It can be a painful bold-faced lie, but that doesn't really make any difference. Even if the truth is eventually discovered, the damage has already been done.

Gossip can also be used as a threat. If you are thinking of straying from the group mentality, the threat of a rumor being spread about you is a peer-pressure ploy used by teens to keep you in step with the rest of the gang. If all of your buds are going to steal candy from the gas station, but you flat-out refuse because you know it's wrong, they might threaten to tell the whole school some nasty untruth about you just to get you to conform. Rather than get a bad rep, you become a thief to save face. It worked, but now you've completely sold out and have been humiliated in a different way—and that's no fun, either.

There's one thing about gossip and rumors that's not all bad: They have an extremely short shelf life. So, if you find yourself suddenly in the unflattering spotlight, don't join the witness protection program just yet. By next week, you will be old news when everybody has moved on to the next juicy tidbit.

What's Everyone Whispering About?

Secrets can be fun, especially if you are privy to them. You feel like you have some insider knowledge that the rest of the world doesn't deserve to know. Secrets can make you feel like a member of an exclusive club, and that confidential info is the password. You have facts in your grasp that are restricted—and, because of that, you have the supremacy of being an insider.

But no one can be an insider all the time, and sometimes you're on the outs. Two of your pals are whispering about something, and you have no idea what they're talking about. You feel completely in the dark, left out in the cold to freeze alone in an information-less tundra. Secrets are no fun now, are they?

Keeping secrets can feel like a very adult thing to do. At one time or another, you must have walked in on your parents who hushed as soon as they saw you, stopping dead in their tracks. Something secretive was going on that they didn't want you to know about. It was frustrating, and you probably mulled it over trying to figure out what the big deal was. Today, you think that secrets of your own make you more grown-up and important.

These hush-hush chats are another way teens make themselves feel good at the expense of others. The most powerful thing about a secret is that you are keeping something from people who want desperately to know what you're saying. Withholding a secret is a form of torture used to let others know that they are not worthy of the restricted information. You can use your privileged status to manipulate a peer into doing exactly what you want. All you have to do is promise to let them in on the mystery.

Kids with a Clue

"I always knew everything about everybody. Then one day I saw my two best friends whispering, and, for the first time ever, I was out of touch. It felt absolutely awful."

—Stephanie, age 15

Ostracizing and Hazing

Chances are, even if you are the most popular person in the whole wide world, you have had moments where you have felt left out. And, boy, are those moments agonizing. Everyone is aware of this feeling, and, unfortunately, teens capitalize on it as a way to snub someone and really hurt their feelings. It started way back in elementary school with birthday parties. Lots of parents insisted that their kid invite the whole class to the party, regardless of whether you were friends, in order to spare feelings. However, some kids had free reign over their guest list, and if you were the one who was left off, you probably spent a Saturday afternoon crying into the pudding that your mom made in a feeble attempt to cheer you up. It didn't help.

Think about the social map of your school cafeteria. Every group has staked out its own table, and there is very little shuffling of the chairs. You might really like that wacky chick in your history class, but her purple hair does not match the letterman jackets in your section. Your clique certainly doesn't want to break bread with her. The truth is, they probably wouldn't be too thrilled about your friendship with her, either. She is an outsider with your group, much like you are one with hers.

Ostracizing classmates who don't match your mold is a common practice. Almost everybody is guilty, to an extent. It's not just the "cool kids" who do the excluding; students of all kinds will reject a nonmember. The end result is always the same. Someone feels bad about themselves, wondering what they did to make people treat them this way. Most never realize that they did nothing.

Hazing is the most severe form of punishment inflicted on teens by their peers. This abuse is mortifying to the victim and sometimes is even physically hazardous. It is embarrassing if you are shoved into your locker by the big boys in front of that sweet girl you've been dreaming about since the fourth grade. You let them do it because you think they'll like you for being a good sport. When it's over, you hope that you guys can hang out.

But if they take it to the next level by torturing or physically harming you, the hazing has gone way too far. These dangerous stunts have led many high schools and colleges to take drastic measures to eliminate the practice of hazing on campus. If students are caught breaking the rules, they risk expulsion and possibly criminal charges.

You Could Be Next

Now, you know the different ways that your peers can apply the pressure with their everyday actions, words, and demeanor. But what if, thus far, you've been free and clear and haven't really been affected by this? You have gone through school virtually unteased and rumor-free. You even feel part of the "in" group. You've somehow managed to avoid these peer-pressure pitfalls. However, before you get too confident, remember that popularity is a fickle friend that can turn on you at any moment.

Straight up, teens can be extremely mean. That is a horrible fact of life, but you have to deal with it. If you're the one dishing out the poison, you probably don't give much thought to your nasty behavior. But any day now, the tables could turn and you could suddenly be the one being teased. Or tortured. Or excluded. You would instantly switch gears and question how anybody could be so contemptible. Just yesterday, you were a part of the gang, the keeper of all the deep, dark secrets. What happened? Maybe the head honchos decided that you were closing in on their turf, or perhaps you had a thought that went against group mentality. Or, there could be absolutely no good reason at all why you're suddenly being treated like a leper. Whatever the cause, you are now among the uncool, the odd man out of a group where you were always in.

Vice Advice

Before dropping one of your friends like a bad habit just because popular opinion has turned on them, put yourself in their soon-to-be-lonely shoes. While this time you are making the decision, next time you might not be so lucky. Someone else could make the decision and leave you in the dust.

It's no fun to suddenly be shunned by your buddies. When their friendship is ripped away from you, it's like losing a security blanket.

These people who were once your entire universe have banned you from their galaxy, and you are now left floating alone through space.

Victim or Villain

It would be just swell if we were super-kind to one another and were all best chums. Life would be just rosy. Well, that ain't happenin'—at least, not until everybody starts making some major changes. And where would be the best place to start? You guessed it, yourself. Begin by answering a few simple questions:

1. Have you ever pushed someone into doing something they didn't want to do?
2. Have you ever teased any of your classmates?
3. Have you ever started or spread a rumor?
4. Do you keep secrets from your friends?
5. Have you ever left anybody out intentionally?
6. Have you gone along with anyone who has done any of these things?

How many of these did you answer "yes" to? If you were guilty even just one time, this makes you one of the bad guys. You showed poor judgment by applying peer pressure and hurt somebody's feelings in the process. You have to change your ways. Think next time before you act. A little brain-to-mouth censoring can save a lot of pain for you and for others.

Being guilty of giving or receiving peer pressure is not always that obvious. Have you ever lied for one of your friends? Let's say that your best gal pal calls you up and wants a tiny little favor. You won't have to do anything, just let her tell her parents that she's spending the night at your house. She's really crashing at her boyfriend's place because his folks are out of town, but her dad would so not go for it, so she's asking for your help. She begs you not to deny her this totally romantic evening; after all, you are her best friend in the world. And she would do it for you. So you cover for her.

You have just been sucker-punched by peer pressure. Lying for your friends is called enabling. You are helping them do something that you know is wrong and that could get you both in big-time trouble. When you do this, you are sending out a message that it is okay for your friends to abuse your relationship and take advantage of the fact that you like them enough to risk getting busted in order for them to have a good time. And you get nothing in this deal except the possibility of getting caught.

Kids with a Clue

"I lied for my friend and said he was studying at my house when really he was at a club in the city. When his mom found out, she told my mom and I was grounded for a week. I didn't even go to the stupid club."

—Lowell, age 13

Being around one of your comrades who is misbehaving is like taking a stroll through a minefield. Imagine that you are witness to the hazing of the nerdy kid in your homeroom. He has just been given his 87th straight wedgie, and there is no end in sight. Everyone in the class is laughing at his obvious pain and humiliation, which only inspires the bully to continue. In your mind, you know that this is really wrong and think of 10 different ways you can put a stop to it. But what do you do? You sit there with your mouth closed and pretend that it's no big deal. Who feels like rocking the boat? You are now just as guilty as the wedgemaster.

But what choice did you really have? You were sure that if you actually stood up in defense of the poor nerd, you would have suffered just as much as he did. You don't want to be thought of as the incredibly uncool one who ruined the fun for everyone else. You didn't really see where you had an option. Sometimes, it's easier to just keep quiet than to speak up for what you know is right.

However, when you don't stand up and defend other people because you are too scared of going against the crowd, you have let peer pressure become your ruler. You may feel like an innocent bystander—technically, you weren't the one doing wrong. However, when you exhibit passive behavior, you are saying, without saying a word, that the name-calling and the insults and the secrets and the lies and the abuse are all okay in your book. Is that the kind of person you want to be? A wet dishrag who lets bullying thugs do their thinking for them? That's not a really slick reputation to have, that's for sure.

The tough guy, or girl, who hurls insults at the speed of light is usually incredibly insecure. Anybody who loads on that kind of pressure probably has a very low self-image. These teens are terrified that their deep, dark secret will be exposed. The meanies hope that no one will ever find out that they're scared of the dark, afraid of spiders, or just plain vulnerable. They dread the tables being turned on them and being called out as a weakling. So, in an effort to defend themselves, they basically make fun of people before others can make fun of them. This is what makes a bully truly pathetic.

The Least You Need to Know

- Teasing is a leftover habit from childhood that teens have not outgrown. It is cruel and immature to mock your peers just because they are different from you.

- Although they're often untrue, gossip and rumors can wreak havoc in an otherwise happy teen's life.

- Even though it's fun to be in on a secret, there is nothing worse than being the one left in the dark.

- During the time in your life when you want so desperately to belong, it is especially painful to be intentionally excluded or harassed by your peers.

- Be careful how you behave and treat others. Bad karma ensures that being nasty will come back to haunt you later.

- Not putting a stop to peer pressure when you have the opportunity makes you just as culpable as the bully.

Chapter 6

Rebel Yell

In This Chapter

- Parental problems
- Dude with a 'tude
- You lie like a rug
- Rules are for fools
- Homework, books, and dirty looks
- Disruptin' the instructin'
- You're beat if you cheat

Following the rules can be harder than breaking them. When you were a kid, you abided by them, for the most part. You might have thought that life was unfair and unjust, and you probably even threw a few temper tantrums in protest. But, in the end, you did what you were told because your parents and your teachers were bigger and older than you. Now, you are a teenager and are ready to strike out on your own, which may cause some dissension in the ranks. In this chapter, we explore your rebellious side and explain why it pays to obey those frustrating rules.

When Mom and Dad Become Them

Breaking the parental chains is a long and arduous process bound to make all those involved want to pull out their hair in frustration. Strangely, when you were a wee pup, you thought that your parents were the coolest people in the world. There was no better way to pass the afternoon than to spend quality time together playing Horsie or Hide-and-Go-Seek. You used to love the way your Dad boogies down to tunes on the radio. And your Mom snorts every time she laughs, which used to send you into hysterics. Those were the good old days that you look back at now with complete and utter horror.

What happened? Why do you feel like your parents have suddenly gone from amazing to annoying? They didn't change; they are still the same dancing, snorting people they always were. But you have. You are no longer an innocent kid. You are now a full-fledged teenager plagued by anxiety, stress, and pressure, and it changes the way you relate to them. These days, it seems to you like every word out of your parents' mouths is spoken with the sole purpose of getting on your last nerve. Your folks are no longer your idols or your role models. They are now the primary source of your embarrassment. They have become the people you can't speak about or to without some sort of snotty tone slipping into your voice.

There is no question that it's totally humiliating to have your Dad belt out a classic disco tune completely off-key while driving you and your pals to the mall. But he's allowed. He is your father, and he deserves some respect. There is no law against bad singing although sometimes it would be nice if there were. And he isn't required to be your chauffeur, anyway. But none of that matters. You feel like his foolish behavior can destroy you socially. Everyone will jump to the conclusion that you are as big a geek as your dad. But, look around—your friends actually like him. They think he's kind of cool in that old-guy-with-a-bald-spot way. You're the only one who wants to tape his mouth closed. Your friends feel the same way about their folks.

Parents—can't live with them, can't send them packing. Everybody is mortified by their folks at one time or another. There isn't a teen out there who thinks that his 'rents are the epitome of cool. Even that Hipster Mom who shops in the juniors department and drives a convertible disgraces her daughter. She wonders why her mom can't be more like her best friend's mom who wears an apron and bakes cookies. With someone else's parents, it may seem like the grass is not only greener, but sometimes the landscaping is better and the dogs don't poop on their lawn. But that's not true. Nobody is entirely thrilled with the parents they've been given, but they're all you've got—sorry, but you can't exchange them for a better model. Make the most of your relationship with them, and keep your complaining and discontent to a minimum. Your folks are trying to do the same.

Kids with a Clue

"I used to refuse to go shopping with my Mom. She was so loud and embarrassing in the dressing room, I just wanted to scream. But one time I was at the mall without her and I saw all these other moms doing the same thing. Now I just let her come and deal with it. After all, she pays when she's there."

—Kara, age 17

Disrespectin' the Pack

When was the last time you went a full week without insulting, disrespecting, or ignoring your family? You probably can't remember that far back, but a good guess is it was sometime before you turned 13. These days, you are chock-full of ideas and opinions that don't always mesh with your parents' school of thought. You lash out, which doesn't help the situation—or the noise level in your house.

Your parents might be quick to blame peer pressure and your pals for your misbehavior. Yeah, it's true that what your buddies say, do, and think is definitely influential and can make you act like a lunatic at times, but in the end you dictate your own behavior. Your folks are having a hard time accepting this. They can't believe that their little angel is making decisions on her (or his) own, let alone (gasp!) decisions that they disapprove of.

And the attitude! Your parents bother you constantly, so you seize every opportunity to be biting and sarcastic back to them, just like you see your friends do to their parents. One of the most overused words in the teenage vernacular—and definitely one of the most obnoxious—is "whatever." Parents hear this a lot since kids think that most of their questions are nosy, irritating, and badly timed, to boot. "Whatever" is guaranteed to fuel fires that are probably already burning pretty brightly on their own.

Lots of teens find it important to stand up to their parents and get under their skin. They feel that it is a great way to express their toughness and individuality and to prove to their peers that they are all grown-up. A common method used is addressing their folks by their first names. Referring to your mother as "Myrna" is a sure-fire technique guaranteed to make her blood boil. By stripping her of her "Mom" title, you are showing no respect to the woman who spent 27 hours in labor before finally having a C-section to bring you into this world. You are completely disregarding the years of love, support, and encouragement that she has given you unconditionally. Calling a person by her first name shows that you are on equal footing. While your parents have always been your biggest supporters, they are definitely not your equals. Nobody is asking you to refer to them as Your Highness—just the respectful Mom and Dad titles they deserve.

Anybody who lives in a house with siblings has heard the scream "Get out of my room!" Chances are, now that you are a teenager, you are the one doing the shouting. Much like when you were two years old, the teen years are a time of mine, mine, mine. You become very possessive of everything within your bedroom walls, and you don't want anybody's grubby little paws anywhere near your stuff. You are also obsessed with your privacy. If your little brother dares to pick up the phone while you are on it or ever logs on to your e-mail account, he will suffer your wrath, probably followed by an angry "Whatever!"

It's not only immediate family who gets on your nerves. There's only one thing worse than spending a day with your Mom, Dad, and baby bro: spending it with them *plus* Granny, Gramps, and all the pesky cousins you've despised since the day they tattled on you for devouring a fudge bomb from the ice cream man an hour before dinner. Family functions have a tendency to bring out the worst in mopey teenagers who make it no secret that they'd rather be polka dancing than at Aunt Nancy's birthday dinner. The best way to get through these dreaded soirées is to grin and bear it. Have faith that your pain and suffering will all be over before bedtime.

Lying to the Folks

Fable has it that first president, George Washington, swore that he could never tell a lie. Well, if that is true, then he must have never been a teenager. If you know any teen who says that he doesn't lie, well, he's lying. And as we were all taught at a very young age, it is wrong to lie. But sometimes you feel like lying is the only way you can stay out of the trouble that you don't want and get into the trouble that you do. Unfortunately, it often backfires, burning you deeper than you ever imagined.

Kids with a Clue

"I told my parents that I was acing geometry, but I was only really getting C's. When report cards came, I tried to change my grade so they wouldn't find out. That worked ... for about a second. They totally knew what was up. I got in so much trouble for all my lying."

—Jayson, age 15

There are all different types of lies on the spectrum. The most common is the straight-up denial of the truth. If Mom asks if you cleaned your room, you answer "yes" even though pigs would turn up their snouts if they got a load of the filth. You have flat-out lied right to her face. You tell Dad that you were in your room all night studying and, of course, that you didn't take the car. Reality check: You spent the evening doing donuts in the supermarket parking lot. Congratulations. You are a big, guilty liar, and you have no shame.

Another method employed by teens to get around telling the truth is creative storytelling. You might casually mention to your folks that you are heading to a small gathering with your nearest and dearest to rent some flicks and eat some harmless pizza. You'd never admit that you are partying with your pals at a raging kegger thrown by some stoner dude whose parents are out of town. You might want to believe that you're less guilty because technically you did mention a bash, but again you are lying through your teeth.

One of the most overused types of deceits is telling a story while leaving out some of the juicier details. You inform your parents that you are going out to dinner with a couple of friends. You just casually forget to mention the fact that the restaurant is also a bar and that you are using a fake ID to get in. Oh, and it's an hour away and your pal's older brother is driving even though he doesn't have his license because he failed his road test a few times. What a cunning little snake you have become.

You might be thinking, "So what, I'm a liar. Who cares? My friends all lie, and it's no big deal." Well, peer pressure has gotten the best of you if that's how you justify your deceitful behavior. But how will that logic help you when you get caught? And you *will* get caught. Parents have a way of knowing these things, of sensing when something's amiss, even if at first it may seem like you have them fooled. It might take days, weeks, or even years, but hold firm to the belief that they will find out. And when they do, you will suffer—big time. Broken trust is difficult to repair.

Breaking House Rules

Most of you probably feel that you are not allowed to run as free as you would like. Wouldn't the world be a fabulous place if you made up the rules? Actually, you'd probably trash most of them, and the first thing to go would be that blasted curfew. It is really cramping your style, having to be in by midnight when everybody else seems to be partying until dawn. And it's not like you come home from an evening out exhausted and fall right into bed, either. Your teenage body is nocturnal, and you're up late anyway. In your mind, it would make a lot more sense to abolish curfews and just come home in time for breakfast. Too bad your parents disagree.

You are a teenager, and things just don't seem to ever go your way. Sorry to say so, but this instance is no different. Curfew is here to stay, and no matter what yours is, you are not going to like it. Even the most lenient parents have kids who think that their clampdown is way too tight. Most teens have a warped perception of other households' rules. Even the fortunate ones often don't realize how good they actually have it. However, some parents really are more strict than others. If you live in one of these high-security homes, you probably feel like the binding restrictions are cutting off your air supply. You feel the need to sing on mountaintops and dance in the streets. If you can't, you just know that you'll go stir-crazy. You need to be free!

So what do a lot of you do? You become escape artists and sneak out of the house or back in whenever you feel like it. Some of you probably know which squeaky floorboards to avoid while fleeing the premises in the wee hours. You can't stand the fact that you are missing out on a party or a game or a hot date with your paramour. So you shimmy down the drainpipe and make a mad dash to the waiting chariot at the end of the block. If you're really daring, you've probably tried to quietly back the car out of the driveway without the engine waking your sleeping folks. You feel like you are being held prisoner without a trial, and breaking out is your only salvation.

Before you totally blow off your curfew or go slinking off into the night, consider the repercussions. If your folks discover your bad behavior, you are going to be so totally busted that you won't get to go anywhere but your bedroom and the classroom for a very long time. And, remember, your parents laid down these laws for a reason. There is nothing scarier for them than thinking about their baby out in the big, bad, creepy world. They can't chain you to your bed although sometimes it may feel like they do. In order to protect you, they just ask that you please respect them and get home when you're supposed to. It will let them sleep much easier. If they can trust you, you will reap the rewards.

Vice Advice

By following your parents' rules, you will gain their trust and confidence. If you make sure that you're in by curfew every weekend, one night when you want an extension to see that awesome concert, you'll have a better chance of convincing them that you are deserving.

Not only do you have to live with their rules, but you are also stuck living with their opinions. Sometimes, you have friends who your folks just hate. They are not willing to listen to you about how great your pal is; their minds are already made up. They don't care that your new amigo is the coolest kid in school and that hanging with him will make your popularity soar. Well, you're not about to drop a bud just because Mom doesn't approve, so you hang out with him on the sly. Very often this occurs in romantic relationships. That boy you are seeing is definitely not the kind you bring home for dinner, and that girl you're into doesn't come close to meeting the parental criteria to be your babe. You are now sneaking around behind their backs. The whole affair just screams Romeo and Juliet.

You're better off being upfront and honest with your parents. If you think your friend is worth going to the mat for, talk to your folks about it and try to get them to give him another chance. However, if you're having some doubts, and your 'rents are dead set against your bond, they might be onto something. Take a look at him from their perspective. You may see that you're better off without him.

Besides the big issues you have with the 'rents, the little ones can be just as annoying. Carrying your weight around the house can seem like it is truly a chore. You are expected to keep your room clean, set the table, take out the trash, and maybe even do some windows. You feel like Mom and Dad had kids just to use them as servants. The way most teens complain and carry on about it, you would think they were playing Cinderella in their own homes. But the truth of the matter is that your responsibilities probably aren't all that extensive. Rather than moan about how life is so-o-o-o unfair because you have to make your bed every morning, just do it and be thankful that your parents don't make you sleep on the floor.

Cutting Loose at School

It's a hard job to have to wake up every single morning before the sun and drag your weary bones all the way to school. You might feel like you could use a little R&R, so you make up your own holiday and take some time off. You know that this is a risky move, but your pals are all skipping out, too, and you just can't face another second of your math teacher droning on about logarithms. You decide to cut out and cut loose.

Missing a class or two might not seem like that huge an issue. After all, you have five days of them a week, for like a billion weeks a year, so a little "vacation" here and there is not a big deal in the grand scheme of things. It's not that you don't think that biology class is important (well, okay, you think it's a waste of time), but you needed a second lunch period to work on your "chemistry" with the cutie you've been scoping. The problem with missing a single class in a day is that it's really hard to carry it off without getting snagged. The school has you on record as being in attendance, and much as you might think that your teacher is clueless, she didn't get her degree without being able to figure out the basics. Or you might just be unlucky enough to run into Mrs. Norris in the hallway only two periods after you bailed out on her literature quiz. It's hard to talk yourself out of that one.

To some, the way to avoid the complications of cutting a class is to take the day off. That way you are guaranteed not to accidentally bump into any of your teachers. It's not like they spend much time at the local arcade. Besides, you've got Dad's signature scrawl down pat, so you can easily forge the note: "Please excuse Dylan from school. He was ill." However, it's not as simple as that. Most schools call home to notify your folks that you were absent. If you live in a small town, your Dad might even see your teacher at the supermarket, and she might ask him how you're feeling. Busted. If you live in a large city, you might have a better shot—or so you think. Word has a way of getting out. Soon the news will get to your parents, who will undoubtedly give you a different kind of vacation: from your social life. Welcome to Suffer City, sweetheart.

Some teens are not cut out for the school thing and feel like academics are just not their cup of tea. They have done about all they can handle and are ready to call it quits. Besides, they can make so much more money if they are pumping gas full-time instead of just after school and on the weekends. With the extra dough they're bringing in, they could get themselves that hot car they've been eyeing. While at first glance this may seem like a sweeter deal than life within those hallowed halls, dropping out of school is never a good idea. It is a decision with repercussions that will echo for years to come. There is a reason why high school lasts as long as it does. If you leave a cake in the oven for half the cooking time, it's going to be mushy and will taste pretty gross. As a student, you are baking in the education oven for a few years and are done only when you graduate. So sit tight and get yourself through. Your friends are right there beside you to share in your suffering.

Pressure Cooker

People who drop out of high school sabotage a lifetime of opportunities. From that point on, they will be perceived as the type of person who quits when the going gets tough (not to mention that they pretty much close the doors on their futures).

Teacher Torture

There's no way around the fact that some classes are just plain boring. Some of your teachers have been giving the same lectures for more than 20 years, and it seems like even they aren't paying much attention. How can anybody expect you to show interest? Some teens figure that a good way to make the school daze more bearable is to be the class clown. They crack jokes and make faces and noises to get the rest of you through those long minutes before the bell, giving them instant popularity. There are definitely times when a jokester is welcomed, but if the learning process is continually interrupted, everyone suffers. Your homework load will multiply, and suddenly that whoopee cushion isn't so funny. And that clown isn't amusing, either.

Sometimes, it's not the comic who disrupts the lesson. Some students take on the role of the bad seed. They are rude and disrespectful to the teacher, and they have absolutely no regard for authority. Many rebels think that this behavior makes them look cool—after all, they are standing up to The Man in front of their peers. They feel like leaders among the oppressed. But high school isn't a union. Nobody benefits when a teacher is too angry and distracted to teach. Keep your mouth closed, and pay attention to what you're being taught. Some of it might come in handy later.

Cheating Yourself Out of a Good Education

In life, you will find that there is often an easy way out of otherwise difficult situations. While sometimes these shortcuts are quite convenient, most times they will take you on a crazy detour and leave you right back where you started, only exhausted, irritated, and usually screwed. Cheating in high school is one of these bad-idea shortcuts. You can pretty much bet your bottom dollar that if you cheat, you are absolutely going to lose.

You know for a fact that your upcoming Spanish midterm is in Señora's desk and that she is in the teacher's lounge siesta-ing. Your grade in her class is dragging down your GPA, and a glimpse would give you the total boost you need. You try to rationalize it: You would still have to memorize a whole bunch of stuff. What is studying, if not memorization? Besides, if you got your hands on that exam and showed it to a few of the right people, your coolness factor would triple. Talk yourself silly, but underneath you are well aware that stealing a test or the answer key is a big no-no. You'll be left without the knowledge that you would have acquired from studying—and if you are caught, there will be a giant red F next to your name in the grade book. Think about what *that* would do to your GPA.

Kids with a Clue

"My parents stole a test when they were in college, and then they sold it. Thirty people, including them, got kicked out because of their screw-up. I would never cheat and be that stupid."

—Brooke, age 16

Just try to tell yourself that it's not really cheating if you let other people copy from you. You know the facts, you did your homework, and you could so easily pass this test. But your buddies are not as prepped as you, and they need to ogle your paper. They try to pressure you by pointing out that they did set you up on that amazing date with the hottie from your rival school, so it's the least you could do to thank them. And, anyway, it makes you feel good to know that you saved their desperate butts. They must think you're the genius of the group; they all sit around and admire the boundless wonder of your intellect. Hello … Earth to you. Don't get too wrapped up in that fantasy world. Your friends just want to pass. If you let them copy, you are all considered cheaters. And if you get caught, you will flunk and waste all that time that you put in studying. It's a dumb move for a smart teen like you.

Maybe you are the one who needs to sneak a peek over someone's shoulder. It's not that you're stupid or don't understand the material; it's just that you didn't have time to study last night because lawnmower racing was on the tube. Nobody could fault you for blowing off your responsibilities to watch the finals, could they? You bet they can. If you are caught looking at the brainiac's test paper, not only are you in deep, but you might pull an innocent classmate down with you just because she had the unfortunate luck of coming directly before you in the alphabet. And she will not take kindly to the fact that you selfishly decided to mess with her perfect record.

Ripping off someone else's work is bound to get you into some big-time trouble. You might think that your teacher has 100 reports to read and that there's no way he would ever know that you plagiarized the encyclopedia. Besides, the edition is so old, your dad used it when he was in junior high. Not wise. For starters, there might be some discrepancies in source material that dated. Also, remember that your teachers are specialists in their fields. They are probably familiar with the references that you use—and they may have even read them. On top of all that, bootlegging an original idea is against the law. Granted, the professional historian might not take you to court over the fact that you ripped off his Civil War essay for your ninth-grade history paper, but he could. The fact that you are a cheat would be on your permanent record. Think hard before you steal an idea. It's never worth it.

The Least You Need to Know

- Your parents may not be the coolest people on earth, but give them a break. They might embarrass you, but everyone else is too embarrassed by their parents to notice.

- Even though you're growing apart from your family, they still deserve your respect. Try curbing your attitude just a little bit every day. It will make life a lot easier for you and them.

- While it might seem like your lies are a means to an end, they could really land you in the doghouse. When you get caught, you lose your credibility and trustworthiness.

- Although you may want to disregard pesky rules at home, they were laid down for your protection. Be a sport and play by them.

- It's hard to get a good education when you don't show up for class. School may seem like a drag, but life without a diploma is even worse.

- Acting out in class might get you a few laughs from the peanut gallery, but undermining your teachers' authority throws off everybody's learning curve.

- Cheating may make things easier for you today, but using a shortcut will only rob you of knowledge that you'll need later in life.

Chapter 7

Getting It On or Putting It Off

In This Chapter

- The word on the street
- It's great to date
- Let's play ball!
- You know it's not your wisest idea if …
- The morning aftermath
- The protection section

To have or not to have sex. That is the question. And it has no easy answers. At some very intense moments, the pros seem to definitely outweigh the cons. The immensity of the decision can sometimes make you long for those simple days when your body wasn't rocked by X-rated yearnings. In this chapter, we look into all the reasons why teens do the deed, want to do it, are afraid to do it, and hold off on doing it.

Let's Talk About Sex, Baby

Ever since that fourth-grade movie about periods and penises, you've been told to wait to have sex. By now, it sounds like a broken CD. It doesn't help that you are also having a really difficult time believing that nobody has sex until they're married. The way your hormones are raging, you can hardly wait another minute, let alone the years until you're "supposed" to walk down that aisle.

The Great Sex Debate can be a doozy. How far are you supposed to go? When are you supposed to do it? Who are you supposed to do it with? There are so many angles to this issue swirling through your mind that it's hard to sort out all the info and emotions.

Most parents are only too happy to chime in with their opinions. Some absolutely forbid their teens from having sex. They have stated clearly and sternly that if you do it, you are disrespecting them and will, in turn, lose their respect forever. As if you didn't have enough pressure already. Other teens have more liberal folks who are not thrilled with the idea but who understand that sex happens and warn their teens to be careful. This open-minded approach is definitely less threatening, but it doesn't make *your* decision any easier.

So where else can you turn for advice? You need some serious, caring, educated opinions from someone who gets it and who's on the level. You don't know anyone like that, so you try health class instead. But there you get nothing but the facts, ma'am. You learn how babies are made—not just the bumping and grinding part, but also the actual biology and medical terminology of sex and the organs. Although it's educational, it's not exactly the guidance you were hoping for, so you continue to search for answers.

Some of you may be wondering what God would think about your struggle. Many teens have always relied on their spirituality to guide them through the rough spots, so they search for signs from a higher power. Most religions follow that "wait" rule and strongly advise holding off on sex until you say "I do." Many believe that premarital fornication is a sin. Although you might be reverent, you are also in the middle of a really close arm-wrestling match with temptation.

You might think, "How wrong or bad can sex really be?" It seems like everyone else is doing it. To hear the guys in the locker room go on and on, it's amazing any of them have the strength to even tell the story with all the action they have supposedly been seeing. But before you let those torrid tales decide your fate, know that most of them—if not all—are lies.

Everyone wants to sound cool. Even the teens you think are cool are trying really hard to seem that way to others. If they think that people will think they're cool, they'll say that they go at it all night long. But the truth is, they are probably just as inexperienced and unsure as you are.

Kids with a Clue

"I was so stressed because it seemed like I was the only person on the planet not having sex. Then, I found out that most of the guys in my group have been totally lying the whole time and they are as big a virgin as I am."

—Joey, age 14

Your significant other is no help, either. This person who you are thinking about sharing one of the most intimate moments in life with is getting so hot and heavy that he will say anything to get you in the mood. Sometimes, your sweetheart will toss declarations of love and devotion or promises to be together for the rest of your lives and then some. He may make you feel guilty by saying, "If you really loved me, you would." If he really loved you, though, he wouldn't put in that position. And your sex-starved lady might tell you that if you don't put out, she knows plenty of guys who will. How are you supposed to decide what is right for you with all this pressure?

Exhausted by your quest for answers and advice about sex, you turn on the TV to escape. Not happening. Practically every channel is filled with beautiful people "making love." Their glistening bodies embrace on beaches and in bedrooms, making it all look very romantic. Characters around your age are doing it like rabbits, and they never suffer any scary consequences for their actions. Why aren't their parents lecturing them like yours are laying it on you? Who's got it right? Who are you supposed to believe?

You are getting tons of mixed signals, but it's up to you to sort them out. The answer can be found only within you.

Vice Advice

People can chime in with their opinions left and right, but ultimately it has to be you and you alone who decides when you are ready to have sex.

Each person has her own alarm clock ticking away inside her body, and nobody's buzzer goes off at the same time. Your best friend may decide to do it at 17 and feel totally comfortable with her actions, but you might feel like you need a few more years. When you're unsure about which choice is right for you, the best and safest plan is to wait. Despite the pressure you get from everybody pushing in both directions, nobody has to live with your decision but you.

The Dating Game

One of the most popular pastimes with both guys and girls is flirting. It is an opportunity to put yourself out there on the dating scene and receive some positive attention. Flirting is basically just talking with a big old smile on your face, some hip wiggling, and some coy batting of the eyes.

Flirting is not exclusive, like most dating. A whole slew of girls might catch your eye, but you're not sure which babe is right for you. So you approach them and tell some of your best jokes to see who's on your page. Communicating with a combination of words and body language gives you an opportunity to feel out the crowd and find yourself a perfect match.

When you were younger, your friends were just that: friends. But now that you are older and somewhat wiser, you are beginning to take a second look at some of your crew and are realizing that some of them are kinda cute—one might even be a potential sweetheart. When you all head out to the movies, you find yourself maneuvering so that you just happen to be sharing popcorn with your new crush. The more time you spend together, the more you realize that you'd like the two of you to be alone.

And so you move on to The Big Date. For the first time, you are in a one-on-one situation without any of the added pressure of your pals watching your every move. However, that's replaced by the pressure to be suave all on your own. You've lost the buffer of your buds filling in the awkward quiet spots, it is up to the two of you to keep the evening rolling along. This is no easy task because you really like each other and want so desperately to make a good impression. You have spent weeks dreaming about this night, and you are going to do all it takes to make things go perfectly. Or so you hope.

Through some miracle, it goes well. You manage not to spill anything on your date or break your nose walking into a wall. Pretty soon the two of you are a couple. The word spreads at school, and, within weeks, your names are combined as one. You are now JenandJason, and all you can think about is each other. This is the feeling you have been hearing about from the other two-headed creature couples. There's no mistaking the rush and intensity. This has got to be love. It's amazing and wonderful and passionate—and surprisingly time-consuming. You can lose whole days just dreaming about your next date and what you will do with your time and with each other.

Let's Get Physical

You once thought kissing was gross, but you are now becoming a die-hard fan. The problem is that kissing doesn't stay just kissing for long. Things can quickly move forward from there. An innocent smooch can lead to third base before you even realize what is happening. You're experiencing new feelings and are having a really hard time letting your brain do all the thinking.

The first thing you must realize is that every feeling you have, no matter how foreign it is to you, is completely and totally natural. All your friends are experiencing the same body-tingling sensations, and while you might not talk about them over ice cream, they are pretty much all that's on anyone's mind. It doesn't matter if you are a guy or a girl; both sexes are feeling those urges coursing through their teenage veins at lightning speed.

Be careful not to let your hormones get the best of you. Make sure that you know exactly what you are getting yourself into. Sex is a big deal. It is a *huge* deal. Deciding when to take the leap from innocence to experience is tough.

You only get one first time. There are no second goes at virginity. Before you give it up, make sure that you understand the value of it. You wouldn't sell your baseball card collection to the first dude who made you an offer, so why should you give the precious gift of yourself to the first warm body that comes along? You will remember your first time for the rest of your life. If you are lucky and smart and play your cards right, it will be somebody who will hold a special place in your heart forever, so don't just settle. You never want to regret your decision, so take a cold shower and hold off until the time is right.

Kids with a Clue

"I almost had sex with this really cute guy at school just because he was cute. But at the last second, I decided that I'd rather wait until I'm in love and it will mean so much more."

—Vanessa, age 16

Suppose that you are absolutely, positively sure that your current squeeze is the *one*. You are head-over-heels crazy about each other, and you can't stand another minute of just touching and groping. You feel that you are ready to take the great plunge and turn your relationship into a sexual one. Make sure that you're positive about this because sex changes everything. A whole new level of intimacy comes along with intercourse. Often, the pressure of that can destroy a once solid relationship. Many adults even have a hard time with this adjustment, so imagine the stress when you are a teenager and it's your first time. It's a lot of new responsibility to take on, and this is a factor that should be considered before you move forward.

You definitely do not want to be wrapped up in the moment and be caught with your pants down—literally. Make sure you have taken the time to talk about it first. A lot of things need to be discussed before you get naked with somebody. Make sure you cover the essentials:

- What is your partner's sexual history?
- What are you going to use for protection?
- Who is responsible for supplying protection?
- What happens if you get (or your girl gets) pregnant?
- How will you deal with it if you catch a sexually transmitted disease?

These questions are no fun. It's not easy to discuss the stuff that's not so lovey-dovey, but you must be open and honest with your partner. Talk about everything that you are thinking and feeling, no matter how hard and embarrassing it might be. After all, if you are ready to go all the way with somebody, you should at least feel comfortable enough to talk to that person about it. And if you're not, consider that as a giant flashing warning sign telling you to call off getting it on.

Every Reason but the Right One

Being madly in love is a good reason to have sex as long as you're totally prepared, know in your head and your heart that you are ready, and are old enough to be able to understand these things fully. But plenty of teens have sex only because of bad reasons. Maybe they don't have a special someone who makes their heart race; they are just positive that they want to have sex, and they want to have it now. Or maybe they are convinced that doing the horizontal hula will make them more popular.

Boys have been hearing for years that all the cool guys have sex in high school. If you are a 17-year-old male virgin, you might feel embarrassed and totally behind the times. Well, relax. Having sex because you think that you're supposed to or so that you'll be popular is way more embarrassing.

It's no different for the gals. If all of your girlfriends are giving it up to their boys, don't feel like you have to be pressured to do so also. If you're not ready, that's totally okay. If anybody tells you otherwise, chances are good that this person is so uncomfortable with her own decision that she wants you to make the same mistakes so she won't feel all alone.

Sometimes, teens are just desperate to get it over with. The anticipation and pressure build and build until they just don't want to deal with it anymore. They feel like they are wearing their virginity like a giant scarlet V on their chest. It doesn't matter where they are or who they're with—they just want to do it and have the first time be history. Too bad it's not as simple as getting into a cold swimming pool: In this case, it's not best to jump right in. Sex is complex and certainly not a decision to be taken lightly. It won't alleviate your stress if you casually sleep with some random person—it will only compound it. Don't sacrifice your virginity just because you're sick of it. When handled with care and maturity, sex is definitely worth the wait.

Having sex does not make you more adult. Only time can do that. You will get there soon enough, so try not to rush things. Plenty of adults don't have sex all the time. They know that when it's not right, it's not right. Being an adult means being mature enough to realize that becoming intimate with a person is a very important decision. If you are really anxious to be a grown-up, start by making grown-up decisions. Decide not to have sex until the time is right.

As if the whole sex issue isn't tumultuous enough, a lot of teenagers are also confused about their sexuality. While their friends are busy checking out the opposite sex, they are busy checking out their friends. These days, homosexuality is not the taboo subject it was when your parents were your age. There are gay role models in the media and probably even in your own hometown who work hard at letting you know that your same-sex sexual preference is totally natural. So don't do what so many teens before you have done and have heterosexual sex just to prove that you are straight. First of all, it will prove nothing of the sort. It will just confirm what you already suspect to be true—that you are gay. Remember, many complex emotions accompany the physical act of sex. To you, doing it may be all about showing how hetero you are, but there is a big chance that your partner thinks that the two of you are in love. You would be responsible for breaking somebody's heart in a feeble attempt to convince yourself of something that you know deep down is a sham.

Kids with a Clue

"My best friend was totally in love with me, and I knew it. All the guys in school wanted her, and she wanted me. We had sex even though I knew I liked guys, and now we're not even friends. I really messed up."

—Alan, age 18

Sometimes, the chaos you are going through both physically and emotionally makes you really crave a little love. But don't fool yourself. *Sex does not equal love!* This concept is hard to grasp at any age, especially for teenagers trying to figure out their place in the world. Some teens may not get the love and support they desire from their family or friends, so they turn to sex as a substitute. Their significant other becomes their one and only, and they allow themselves to become consumed by the relationship. Some even take it a step further and conceive babies to give themselves someone else to love. Before you throw caution to the wind and become a teenage pregnancy statistic, squeeze yourself into the baby's booties. Would you want to be the kid born out of desperation? It's not fair to you or the child.

Life's not fair, especially when things don't go your way. Breaking up is hard to do. That is why there are so many love songs about heartache and misery. The process of unmeshing yourself from the person who had become your other half is painful and torturous. You just have to yell and scream or cry or do whatever it is you need to do to get yourself through the gloom. But one thing you should never do is use sex to hold on. Lots of teens are convinced that if they give their sweetheart the gift of sex, they can get back to those blissful days they used to share. But sex is not a problem solver. In fact, it is just the opposite. When you use sex as a last-ditch effort to cling to a broken relationship, you are selling your mind and your body short and are asking for your heart to be broken all over again.

Don't let pressure be the reason you go all the way. It might be really hard to say no to your sweetie when your body seems to be shouting yes, but if there is any doubt, bail out. You have the right to say no at any time. You might be only a millimeter from the big moment, but if you suddenly change your mind, that is totally cool and your partner had better stop. If he doesn't, that is rape. It doesn't matter that he's your boyfriend and he says he loves you; when he forces sex on you after you've said the magic word "No," he has stepped over the border into the land of illegal. It doesn't even matter that the two of you have done it hundreds of times before. Every single solitary time stands on its own, and you get to choose whether you want to have sex. Don't ever succumb to the pressure placed on you by a horny partner. Stand your ground and know that your body is your property; anybody who wants admittance has got to play by your rules.

Dealing with the ConSEXquences

Sometimes, you get caught up in the moment and all logic and reasoning gets thrown out the window. The here and now feels so mind-blowing that you don't care about anything. Earthquakes, tornadoes, and hurricanes could hit, and you wouldn't even notice. You want this now, and you will deal with consequences later. They couldn't be that huge, could they? After all, how could something that feels this good bring on something bad?

Oh, it can, in many ways that you'd never want to experience. The repercussions of sex can be huge, and the odds are not stacked in your favor. Maybe you are one of the lucky ones and the only thing that comes out of your experience is a naughty reputation. Because even if you and your partner are deeply in love and have promised to keep your passion private, sex has a way of becoming public knowledge. It may be done unintentionally, but most teens are bursting at the seams to share their encounters with their nearest and dearest. Unfortunately, their pals are just as eager to talk about it, and before you know what's happened, the whole school knows about what you did Wednesday night, right down to the song that was playing on the radio. Now, imagine the gossip if you two aren't a couple—you just got busy at a party last weekend. Sweet Caroline is now Tart Caroline.

Perhaps, you are a guy who dreams of having a reputation as a ladies' man. Before you start prowling on your quest to become a full-fledged stud, you might want to stop and consider how macho you'll feel when you're changing poopy diapers at 2:00 in the morning. That's right, surprise! Sex brings pregnancy, so bid farewell to your life as a Casanova.

Pressure Cooker

The younger you are, the more fertile you are. Girls in high school who have unprotected sex even once have an almost 70 percent chance of becoming pregnant.

Are you ready to be a parent? You might think it doesn't sound like that hard of a job—after all, your parents are spazzes, and they do it. But babies seriously curb your social life. You can't just go out to the movies, or the game, or even the store without thinking about who is going to take care of Junior. And babies need food and diapers and always have to go to the doctor, none of which comes cheap. Somehow, your after-school job at the record store just does not seem like the financial goldmine you once thought it was. Think about the life changes you'll have to make before you get carried away by that five minutes of physical pleasure.

If this isn't enough to make you think hard before climbing into the sack with your amore, consider that you also might be given the lovely gift of a sexually transmitted disease. More than 20 different kinds of STDs out there are just waiting to nest in your goods. These critters have names like gonorrhea, syphilis, chlamydia, genital warts, and herpes. They don't exactly sound friendly, do they? They're not.

Some are curable with medication, but many are barely controllable. They may go away temporarily, but they can come back to haunt you for the rest of your life. And you have to worry about passing them to other people. STDs have been linked with birth defects, sterility, blindness, and even cancer. It's a huge price to pay for a few moments of gratification.

If all this isn't terrifying enough, there's always HIV and AIDS to scare the heck out of you. AIDS has deadly consequences and is not exclusive in choosing its victims. Anyone can contract it and there's no way to tell who's infected without a blood test. It's hard to believe that one roll in the hay can change your life forever, but it can. So be careful and don't take chances with your health. No sex is worth the risk.

So You've Decided to Do It

You've weighed the good and the bad. You know all about disease and pregnancy, about the emotional responsibilities and the value of your virginity. You are well informed and have talked about everything with your partner. The two of you have decided that you're going to go through with it.

Oh, wait. One more thing. Have you decided what method of birth control you are going to use? Make sure you choose wisely. Lots of foolish myths are floating around the hallways, and you wouldn't want to be misled. Here are some methods that do absolutely nothing to protect you:

- Standing during sex
- Jumping up and down when you're finished
- Coughing and sneezing to expel the sperm
- Peeing after you're done
- The classic "pull out and pray"

Just to make things very clear, none of these silly old wives' tales works—not even a little bit. Sperm can travel whether you're standing on your head or lying on your back. And once it enters your body, nothing can flush it out. Pulling out before ejaculation might sound like a good plan, but some sperm-containing semen always sneaks out before climax, and it takes only one sperm to make a baby.

Kids with a Clue

"I heard that you can't get a girl pregnant the first time you have sex. My girlfriend and I now have a 2-year-old to prove that theory wrong."

—Matt, age 18

If you are going to have sex, make sure you're smart about it—use protection. Some teens don't because they are afraid that their parents will find it and will totally bust them. No, the folks would probably not be thrilled to find your nightstand filled with condoms, but they would be way more upset if they had to help raise your child. Your religion might forbid birth control, but it also probably forbids teenage sex, so that excuse is useless, too. Some might argue that it ruins the moment, and it's so unsexy to slip a rubber hat on the manhood. Remember, the potential consequences are even less sexy. It's easy to make sex safe. Using protection is not a big deal, so stop being dramatic and play it smart.

The most common and widely used form of protection is the condom. Condoms are affordable and are sold in drug stores. Also, many schools and health clinics give them out for free. Not only do they help prevent pregnancy, but they are also effective against many STDs. But condoms are not foolproof. And even brand-new condoms can break, so be careful.

Birth control pills have a high success rate at preventing pregnancy if they are taken every single day without fail. But if you miss even one day, your risk factor skyrockets. Plus, the pill will do absolutely nothing to keep you from getting a disease, so it's best when used along with a condom.

Diaphragms are used to block the cervix so that the sperm cannot enter and impregnate the egg. The problem with them is that they are often messy and difficult to insert, not to mention that they too do nothing to ward off disease. Neither do depo shots or spermicides. They are all solely for the purpose of preventing pregnancy. And none of these is completely effective.

The only sure-fire method of birth control and disease prevention is abstinence. You can't get in trouble if you don't do the deed. Ultimately, the decision is yours. Just make it an educated and well-thought-out one.

The Least You Need to Know

- Everyone has a different opinion about the right time to have sex. The only opinion that matters to you is your own.

- Now that you're in high school, you are experiencing the excitement of dating. You may find yourself in love, but be informed and beware before you take the next step physically.

- Having sex is not a decision to be taken lightly. Weigh all the factors carefully, and don't let your raging hormones make the decision for you.

- Make sure that your reasons for entering into the world of sex are the right ones. Don't let pressure push your buttons and push you into doing anything you're not ready for.

- Sexual experiences are not easily forgotten. There are repercussions to everything you do, and the aftermath of sex can change your life forever.

- If you feel that you've found the right time, right place, and right person, and you want to make the leap, take the proper precautions to protect yourself. Prevention saves a lot of time, energy, and emotional turmoil later.

Chapter 8

Drinking, Drugs, and Disillusionment

In This Chapter

- If I hear "Just say no" one more time ...
- Ignoring the lectures
- Pills, thrills, and ills
- Gateway to disaster
- The stoner tax

We all know that smoking causes cancer and that drugs are evil. It makes you wonder why people still do them. Substance abuse continues to be a major problem across the world. And what age group do you think is guilty of comprising a large part of the statistics? You guessed it—teenagers. The teen years are a time of curiosity and experimentation. Unfortunately, curiosity killed the cat, and it could kill you, too. In this chapter, we'll evaluate the reasons people try drugs, what they do to your body, and how you'll pay for using over and over again.

Blah, Blah, Blah, Tell Us Something We Don't Know

Practically since the day you were born, you started hearing the warnings. The "Just Say No" campaign in the 1980s, started by then–First Lady Nancy Reagan when husband Ronald was in office, had that slogan plastered everywhere. It was a major step taken to battle the war on drugs that had claimed so many lives and still continues to do so.

By now, we are all well aware of the evils of drinking, smoking, and drugs. They teach this in schools, community centers, places of worship, and even work environments. These anti-everything messages are hurled at us constantly. We hear them so often that we suffer from complete and total overkill. Lectures, lectures everywhere. What's a teen to do? You understand—it's loud and clear, thank you very much. You feel like shaking your fists at the sky, yelling, "Okay, drugs are bad. I get it. Can we please move on?"

For a while, the messages worked. When you were a kid, it was probably second nature to wriggle your nose disapprovingly if you saw someone smoking even if the person was a member of your own family.

The antismoking commercials on TV were so disturbing that you probably had nightmares after catching one between your cartoons. And what about booze and dope? You were taught—and agreed with the fact—that people who drink or take drugs are just losers. They are the ones who get kicked out of school and fired from jobs. Next thing you know, they end up sleeping in the park and begging for change with two different shoes on. It's a nonstop train to Loserville, and you didn't want to be anywhere near the station.

Now, you're way older than you were the first time you were warned about this stuff. You always heard that lots of people took drugs, but now you actually know some of them. You may have even tried some of these bad-news behaviors yourself.

All of a sudden, the rules don't seem as cut and dried as they did when you were a kid. Drugs may not seem as bad to you now or as big of a deal. After all, the kids you know who do them aren't degenerates. They aren't necessarily getting expelled or arrested. Come to think of it, they're a lot like you.

Kids with a Clue

"My dad used to smoke cigarettes like crazy when I was a kid. I really wanted him to quit, so every time he lit up, I faked a massive coughing attack. I guess it worked 'cause he hasn't smoked in six years. Man, did he freak when he found a pack in my room."

—Joey, age 14

Why Would You Start?

If doing drugs is bad Bad BAD, then what the heck would make anyone in his right mind ever go near the stuff? Taking drugs is a learned behavior, and there are many places from which to learn. It's human nature to copy what you see—and, unfortunately the bad comes along with the good.

Although many teens partake in these vices, drinking, smoking, and drugs are usually associated with adults. As a teen, you feel like you're almost an adult yourself. You're a 50-cent cab ride away from being a full-fledged grown-up. And you may be in a huge rush to get there. When you were a child, you couldn't wait to become a teenager. Now that you're a teenager, you can't wait to become an adult. (Oddly enough, adults don't want to be senior citizens—they want to be kids. Try figuring that out.)

Some teens think that taking drugs makes them look older, which is, of course, totally ridiculous. First of all, a teenager looks like a teenager. If you're smoking, you look like a teenager smoking, and that's it. And why would anyone want to look like an adult who does that junk anyway? Those adults look purely pathetic.

Even though teens know the dangers of drugs, something inside makes them do stupid things they never thought they'd do. Here comes the influence of peer pressure again, and it's taking no prisoners. It's powerful, and it pushes people smack into the middle of busy streets.

Drugs are a popular pastime within certain peer groups. If you want to hang out with one of these groups, you may feel like you have to do as they do. Maybe one of the cool kids made a rude comment when you didn't have a drink in your hand. It made you squirm uncomfortably, so to avoid a repeat performance of that humiliation, you make sure that you always have an ice-cold brew on you from now on. But the pressure doesn't have to be that straightforward to be forceful. If all your pals are smoking cigarettes, how do you feel being the only one who doesn't know how to blow a smoke ring? Even if they don't say anything about it to you, you may still feel like you should light up just so that you don't stand out in the crowd. Sometimes, it isn't that easy to "just say no."

The teen years are an experimental time. You're getting used to a whole new you: new body, new thoughts, new attitude, new friends. There's so much bombarding you that you have to put all your energy into digesting this fresh information. It's hard to figure it all out, so you're taking your time and trying to get comfortable in your own skin. You're not sure who you really are—or even who you want to be—so you test the waters to see where you stand. After all, if you want to find out what your thing is and what you're really into, you have to try a lot of different stuff to figure out what suits you. And sometimes you make mistakes.

You probably spend a lot of time questioning authority. You feel bound by rules that you don't understand and definitely don't agree with. It frustrates you, so you lash out. The teen years have always been an infamous time for rebelling. Your parents say "hot," you say "cold." Your teacher says "stop," you say "go." This feeling of conflict often drives teens to try drugs as a way to stick it to their elders. Although they know that it's bad for them, they want to be bad, they want to be dangerous, and they may even want to get in trouble. This sounds insane, but it is a very real reaction to the tumultuous, confusing feelings that are going on inside.

Vice Advice

You may think that taking drugs is a great way to make your parents suffer. While this is true, remember that the person you're hurting most is yourself.

Growing up is tough, and most of the time it feels like it's only getting tougher. You're stressed out and exhausted, like the weight of the world is on your shoulders. Being a teen should be a blast, but lately your life is the farthest thing from fun. Your days are filled with endless cycles of ups and downs, like you're stuck on an elevator with a 5-year-old controlling the buttons. You have a lot on your mind. Your head is swirling with issues that you either don't want to deal with or don't know how to deal with. A lot of times you feel kind of out of it, and you're not even sure why. Sometimes, you just wish that you could forget about everything and tune out even if it's just for a little while.

Drugs can be a strongly tempting, though dangerous, means of escape. And they do serve that purpose very well. Drugs can totally whack you out, to the point that you might not know where you are or even who you are. You forget your problems for the moment. You forget almost everything. For a couple of hours you may feel elated, almost like a different person. You can't believe you had any worries at all. They seem so unimportant when you're under the influence.

Too bad the problems are still there when you sober up. Drinking and drugs may temporarily relieve your pain, but the problems aren't going anywhere. You just tricked yourself into forgetting for a little while. The next morning, you're staring at the same issues that plagued you the night before, only this time with a raging hangover. Now, you have to deal with a splitting headache on top of everything else.

Unfortunately, even if you try your hardest to stay away from drinking, smoking, and drugs, you can't help the fact that these things are still all around you, everywhere you look. Thank the media for that. It's a powerful influence that has a stronger presence than you realize. We are surrounded constantly with images of the party life: on television, in movies, in ads in magazines, and on larger-than-life billboards. We are bombarded by messages that aren't necessarily positive—or even remotely true.

Anyone can post a billboard or shoot a commercial. You just need to shell out the cash. Then all of a sudden, voilà! Your message, no matter how detrimental, is posted high and large for all to see. Even advertising poison is obviously legal. You've seen the cigarette ads of those phony girl-power posers puffing away, haven't you? And that billboard near the Quicky Mart, the one with those hot guys and girls enjoying their fancy cocktails, is hanging in a hundred other cities for a hundred-thousand other teens just like you to see. The people in the ads are doing the things that we were taught were bad, but they look like they're having a blast. What's up with that?

Well, the big boys in the ivory towers of these companies would love it if they could convince you to start smoking and drinking. They figure that by illustrating how much fun doing it is through these ads, consumers will bite and open their wallets. They think they can manipulate you. How dare they! Do they really think that you're that impressionable? Well, yes. They bank on it, and they buy their big houses and fancy cars because of it. But you don't have to be a sucker. Just make the decision to stay away from drugs—and stick to it.

What's Your Poison?

Cigarettes are the number-one killer drug in the United States today. Cigarettes contain nicotine, which is an addictive drug that keeps people smoking. Even though warnings are everywhere, people still light up. And teens are especially guilty. Although it's illegal for minors to buy cigarettes, cigs are fairly easily accessible.

Smoking will considerably shorten the smoker's life span. Cigarette smoking strains the heart by forcing it to work harder, and it also tightens your blood vessels. Smokers have difficulty breathing because cilia in the lungs, which sweep out dirt and unwanted particles, become clogged. This causes severe coughing. Cigarettes are the leading cause of heart disease, which is the number-one cause of death in the United States. Smoking weakens the blood's ability to carry oxygen, which affects the function of your muscles and liver.

Still interested? Okay, then consider this: Smoking costs hundreds of dollars a year. It turns teeth and fingers yellow and makes hair, breath, and clothes smell. Smokers prematurely age and get wrinkles, and they also suffer from lung and mouth cancer, gum disease, and heart attacks. Yum!

The good news about the smoking issue is that fewer people are lighting up these days than in the past. Numbers have dropped off considerably, partially because of laws and taxes that have raised the price of cigarettes. It is also becoming more difficult to find a place to smoke. Many offices and public areas forbid or restrict it, and restaurants are quickly following suit. How nice to be able to enjoy your chili cheese fries without the suffocating aroma from some joker's cancer stick.

Alcohol is a widely used drug that people often forget is a drug at all, probably because it is accepted and legal in today's society. The fact that it is a serious substance that can be deadly is often overlooked. Many people begin experimenting with alcohol during their teenage years. Because drinking is such a popular practice, they choose to ignore the fact that this is an unhealthy habit to start—and illegal when done underage.

You might be thinking, "So what? There are plenty of things that are illegal and so much worse. What's so bad about a wine cooler or a kamikaze shot?" You've heard about the hangover thing, but way before you even get to that point, you'll probably be affected by nausea and vomiting. You'll swear that if the world just stops spinning, you'll never have a drink again. Your wish is granted, and the next night you're back to normal. Hopefully, your short-term memory is still intact, and you don't pick up another drink for a repeat performance of the night before.

Kids with a Clue

"I spend every Friday night partying hard with my friends. But it always ends the same. I always end up spending more time kneeling in front of the 'porcelain god' than sleeping. Totally wrecks the rest of my weekend."

—Matt, 18

Drink enough, and you could get liver and kidney damage. Or, if you're lucky, ulcers. And did you know that alcohol greatly slows down nerve cells, retarding your coordination and thinking? You're going through puberty; you don't need to be any more awkward. Excessive drinking will also slow growth. That's more good news for short people. As an added bonus, alcohol can cause cirrhosis, pancreatitis, gastritis, and cancer of the esophagus as well as brain damage. Quick, tap the keg and let the diseases flow.

Marijuana, also known by common names such as "pot," "weed," and "grass," has long been popular among young people. Marijuana is a mood-altering drug made from the hemp plant. It may make you feel mellow, but actually you are experiencing an increased heart rate. You'll become paranoid, lose motivation, have difficulty focusing, and develop a lack of concentration and comprehension. Toking up can cause throat damage and eventually lead to lung disease similar to that caused by cigarettes. Du-u-u-ude … that sucks. Teens who get into this drug will often lose the friends they had before they started because they would rather hang out with other potheads moving at the same slow pace.

Cocaine, called "coke" for short, is a much harder drug than marijuana. It comes in two forms: white powder and crystals. Cocaine in the crystal form is called crack. Coke is snorted, while crack is smoked. The user of cocaine experiences a quick high—and an even quicker crash. Crack is more concentrated; its high lasts only for 5 to 10 minutes but is followed by an intensely hard crash. Users want to get back "up," so they take more, starting a vicious cycle. This is exactly how all-consuming addictions begin.

Pressure Cooker

Smoking marijuana can be extremely dangerous when taken with alcohol. The physical and mental effects are magnified, which can totally mess you up.

Continued snorting of cocaine can make holes in the septum between the nostrils deep inside your nose, but it's not like piercing—there is no place to put a ring. Both coke and crack increase blood pressure. Taking them can cause major depression, insomnia, panic attacks, and hallucinations. They can lead to brain seizures and often cardiac arrest, which can cause death. Habitual users are not the only ones who jeopardize their lives. Death can occur the first time the drug is taken. Then, there are no second chances.

Amphetamines are stimulants or "uppers" while barbiturates are depressants known as "downers." They both come in pill form or powder, which is shot up (injected). While uppers do produce a powerful high, it's accompanied by confusion and insomnia (an inability to sleep). If you take them, you can have brain damage and heart attacks. Mix them with alcohol, and you've guaranteed yourself a hospital stay. Barbiturates have the opposite effect. They'll put you into a dreamy, relaxed state, but beware the withdrawal—it is a living nightmare. This drug will slur your speech, make you nauseated, and slow your reflexes. You may even suffer from double vision and a lack of balance, which can make even the simplest task impossible. Then, in the worst-case scenario, you'll face massive convulsions and possibly death. Talk about a downer.

Inhalants are especially dangerous because of their easy accessibility and high toxicity. You probably have some of them in your own house right now and don't even know it. Fumes given off by household products can be inhaled to make you high. This process, known as "huffing," produces a sensation similar to drunken intoxication. You get dizzy and confused, and you may hallucinate and become aggressive or violent. Substances such as glue, paint, and gasoline produce these types of fumes. It's hard to believe, but people actually think it's a good idea to sniff glue. Talk about pathetic.

Hallucinogens are known as "psychedelics." The "it" drug in this set of vision-inducing substances is lysergic acid diethylamide, also known as LSD or "acid." Psychedelic mushrooms, also called "magic mushrooms" or "shrooms," are a close relative of LSD. Also in this dysfunctional family is phencyclidine, better known as PCP or "angel dust." These drugs were all the rage in the drug culture of the 1960s, and their popularity continues today. Some teens have a romanticized view of those hippie days and drop acid to try to re-create a sense of that time. They experience an altered mental state called a "trip," which is sometimes beautiful and thought to be "mind-expanding." However, like crappy vacations where planes are delayed and luggage is lost, all drug trips are not so rosy. Some can be terrifying and panic-inducing. Flashbacks can happen for years afterward even if you try LSD only once. You might be forced to experience a bad trip repeatedly. This may sound like a severe sentence for a one-time crime, but sometimes when you trip, you're bound to fall.

Use these bad beauties, and you can expect to experience violent moods and extreme mood swings. You'll be afraid of your own shadow and terrified of anybody else's. Your memory will be shot and so will your power of speech. You'll feel dizzy and nauseated, which goes great with the tremors. You'll have a complete loss of physical and mental control—and possibly even heart and lung failure. Now does this sound like a trip worth taking? Didn't think so.

Aaah, heroin. This is the granddaddy of the illicit drugs. Plainly put, it is the most devastating and damaging drug around. Derived from the opium poppy plant, heroin is incredibly expensive, and an addiction is guaranteed to break the bank. And once you're a junkie, you're a junkie for life. This puppy can be snorted or shot with a hypodermic needle. If it's injected directly into the vein, it's called "mainlining." Eventually, veins collapse from over-injection. If you share a needle, you move into a high-risk group for contracting HIV. It sounds so awful, why would anybody do it? Well, heroin provides a powerful high along with a very relaxed feeling and a sense of relief. Good, right? Wrong! Users take increasingly larger doses in an attempt to feel as awesome as they did that first time, but this never happens. Eventually, there's no high at all—but by this point, the user has developed an incredibly strong addiction and is a slave to the needle. Breaking this beast of a dependency is an extremely difficult process. The withdrawal is physically and mentally excruciating. No high is worth that low.

Teens also get into lots of other types of drugs, sometimes completely innocently. They may not realize the severity of their behavior or understand that taking these drugs could be deadly. They just think it's something to do to have fun, like going to the movies or getting ice cream. Drugs like ecstasy, known as "X," have become a super-popular part of some party scenes. If a person tries a drug like this once and has a good time, chances are good that she'll do it again, in total denial that she is gambling with her life.

Kids with a Clue

"I had a friend who tried X at a party. Well, it definitely had something else in it because she started having seizures and had to be rushed to the hospital. The doctor said she almost died."

—Ally, age 15

A scary thing about doing drugs, besides all the scary things we already mentioned, is that you never really know what else is mixed in with your drugs. Very few illicit drugs are pure; many are cut with other substances to save the drug dealer money. After all, he is a businessman. Do you think he's worried about your health and safety? Let's guess no. You may end up ingesting some totally freaky stuff that's even worse than the stuff you thought you were getting. These situations can lead to overdoses, other extreme physical traumas, and possibly even death.

You can never know what any of these drugs will do to you personally; everyone is affected differently. Some people can use a drug for years and never have a violent reaction. Others can try a tiny bit once and end up in the hospital or dead.

A Step in the Wrong Direction

You may be thinking that we gave you a totally dramatic lesson about the big bad drug wolf. You've heard it all before. And you're a smart person. You're aware of your own situation and are careful about what you do and how you do it. Maybe you don't think it's a huge deal to have a brewski once in a while or to take a drag off a joint occasionally. And, honestly, this sort of behavior is not full-blown drug abuse, not by a long shot. But certain substances are known as "gateway" drugs. This term is usually given to cigarettes, beer, and marijuana. They are called this because they often act as a gateway for the user to try more dangerous drugs. They are considered less serious and intense than the harder stuff. What seems fairly harmless can sometimes be the first step in a much worse direction even when taken in moderation.

Obviously, drinking a beer is nothing like shooting heroin. So how could anyone logically think that one behavior can lead to another? The two don't even seem related. It's true, smoking a joint here and there won't necessarily put you on some horrendous path to crack addiction. But the truth is, once you start taking drugs—even mild ones—soon you're thinking that the heavy hitters aren't such a big deal anymore.

Let's use smoking as an example. You used to think that smoking was a ridiculous thing to do. Really, lighting a dead plant on fire and inhaling the smoke? It sounded like something that would maybe happen accidentally if you were building a campfire. You'd probably throw water on it. Actually doing it on purpose would be insane. But a few months ago you shared a cigarette with your friend at a party. You coughed a couple times and actually felt a little dizzy.

Then the next weekend, you shared another one. This time, it felt smoother and you kind of thought you looked like a cowboy. You looked in the mirror and struck a pose: "Hmmm, I look cool with a capital C." After that, you had your own cig once in a while at a party or after you went out for pizza with your friends. Before you know it, you're buying packs and saving the little UPC symbols off them to order free stuff that you don't need. You're hooked, but it doesn't feel like that big of a deal. People everywhere are doing it, too, which makes it seem all the more normal.

Now that you're used to smoking, you realize that the group you partied with isn't always puffing away on cigarettes. Joints are being lit up and being passed around. So you take a hit off one. After all, it looks practically the same as a cigarette; you figure it'll probably feel the same, too. But it doesn't. You get high. Now, you don't think twice about taking a puff of a joint. You even learn how to roll your own. You've started on the path to drug use, and you barely even noticed.

What happened was that you got over the hump. You never intended to try smoking, and you managed to stay away from it for years. Then, on that fateful night, you took that fateful drag that led you to use a more serious drug. Every foray into experimentation knocks down another barrier.

There's No Such Thing as a Free High

We've covered the health ramifications of taking drugs, but there are many other ways that this reckless behavior can lead to trouble not only for yourself, but also for others. Let's start by reiterating the fact that drugs are illegal. And the few drugs that are legal, such as cigarettes and alcohol, are not legal if you're underage. Laws vary from state to state, but there are repercussions for underage drinking that are not fun to deal with.

Partaking of any drug on school grounds is strictly forbidden. Teachers love to bust kids smoking in the boys's room or behind the bleachers. Obviously, drinking and other drugs are also not allowed, so think before you and your buddies decide that it would be a total blast to go to class stoned. It won't be so funny when they expel you or, worse yet, call your mom.

Kids with a Clue

"My friend Grant and I shared a locker, and he had some pot in there. During a random locker check, they found the stash and we both got suspended. It was so not fair."

—Greg, age 16

Just having illegal drugs on you can be the ticket for a total legal disaster. Possession can lead to jail time, no questions asked. Try telling a police officer that you're holding it for a friend, and he'll probably laugh at you. Then, he'll cuff you.

Trouble with the law is bad enough, but being responsible for the death of another person is an infinitely more tragic burden to bear. Drunk driving kills innocent people every day. The people who drive drunk aren't necessarily losers who downed a case of beer and then hopped in the car to go get more. Sometimes, they are people like you who have had a couple of beers with their burgers. Their judgment was a bit off, and the result was a fatal accident. Now, besides the legal issues, they have to live the rest of their lives knowing their carelessness caused another person's death. Remember this fact and burn it into your brain: If you do decide to have a drink, make sure you stay away from the wheel.

The Least You Need to Know

- The anti-drug lectures that you constantly hear can be annoying, but it doesn't hurt to pay attention anyway. After all, they make an important point.
- Lots of factors contribute to why people decide to take drugs. Understanding them and keeping them in mind will help you resist the temptation.

- Each drug has a very different effect on the body and mind. All are dangerous in their purest forms, and they can be even deadlier if they're mixed or cut with another substance. The facts are frightening, so take time to learn exactly what these drugs are capable of.

- You may think that using drugs (like cigarettes and alcohol) is not a big deal, but getting used to them can put you on a path to more dangerous behavior in the future.

- The consequences of taking drugs are numerous and far-reaching. If you let yourself get pushed into playing with fire, be prepared to get burned.

Letting the Air Out: How to Deal with Peer Pressure

If you've been doing your reading, at this point you know pretty much everything about the beast that is peer pressure. But now we're going to tell you how to deal with it—and even make it work to your advantage.

In the final three chapters, you will learn some great ways to defeat peers who pressure before they get the best of you. We'll also show you how sometimes even this dark cloud can have a silver lining. Finally, you'll learn where and how to get support and how to give it to friends in need. So, turn the page and get started taming the peer pressure beast!

Chapter

Standing Your Ground While Keeping Your Cool

In This Chapter

- Building boundaries
- Keep your distance, Bub
- No, thank you, and other methods to avoid the mayhem
- Hustle your muscle

Peer pressure can fight hard, and it can fight dirty. Sometimes, the punch is stronger than a heavyweight contender on steroids. If you don't know how to brawl, you'll be knocked out and headed for the mat before you can say "Ouch!" And you don't have to be flat on your back to know when you've got to work on your technique, either. You need some lessons on how to deal, how to defend yourself, and how to stand your ground. In this chapter, you'll learn some tactics that will help you stay on your feet—and, ideally, out of the ring altogether—when you're up against peer pressure.

Knowing Your Limits

You try to be cool. You try hard. You're preoccupied with the concept, but you may not really understand the meaning of the word in its entirety. Many teens put lots of importance on superficial stuff like looks, clothes, and how they appear to their pals. They think that if they are attractive to others, the clouds will part, the birds will sing, and life will be perfect. Too bad it's not that simple. The only way to get happy is to improve yourself from the inside out and to make peace with your personality and your true self. Teenagers spend so much time worrying about what others think that they forget to work on their Inner Cool.

You show people only the parts of you that you want them to see. You are the lone soul who knows what's really going on inside. There is probably stuff that you are happy with or at least can deal with. That's the you that you display to the world. But everyone has stuff that they're not too thrilled about. You keep those things buried deep inside. Maybe you're embarrassed about them or don't think that they fit other people's definition of "cool." Whatever your reason, it's totally okay to keep things private until you've worked out the kinks.

Whether it feels like it or not, you are an amazing person unlike anyone else in the whole world. You don't fit into any category because they're all too limiting for you. You can do anything that you put your mind to if you try hard enough and don't let anyone ever tell you otherwise. Yeah, yeah, we know, this sounds like a pep talk. But, come on. Doesn't everyone need a pep talk once in a while? You need to remind yourself that you rock because strength and confidence will help you through the rough spots.

The tumultuous teen years are tough enough to throw anyone into a tailspin. You're up, you're down, you're hot, you're cold, and those things switch at the drop of a hat. When the wind changes direction, your emotions are turned inside out and backward.

Vice Advice

Life may seem difficult now, but it gets easier as you grow into yourself and become the good, smart, caring individual you are destined to be.

Think about yourself and who you are and who you want to be. Dig down inside—deep down, in your guts and in your head. Consider how you really feel, and think about the world around you. You're taught morals by your parents, by your teachers at school, and maybe even by your religion. But now that you're growing up, you're formulating your own ideas. You're thinking more in depth about stuff that you always just quietly accepted when you were a kid.

This is a sign of growth and maturity. Keep it up! Question everything you are told. Yes, rules and laws are set for a reason: to protect people and keep things in general order. But besides that stuff, think about why the world works the way it does. Why are you taught certain lessons? Why are certain ways of thinking just accepted? It's almost like some customs have just gone on for so many years that people forget why they started in the first place. Don't blindly accept what people tell you. Think about it and formulate your own opinions. When you do, you will be well on your way to developing your Inner Cool.

As you evaluate the world, you develop your own rule book. Be a sponge and learn all you can about everything, and then make your own evaluations. Armed with knowledge, confidence, and self-respect, you are more than ready to decide for yourself what's right for you. Have pride in yourself, how you look, what you do, what you're into, how you behave, and what you're all about. You are a good person who makes good decisions, and no one makes them better for you than you.

Think everything through and develop your own stances on issues such as drugs and sex and rebelling. This is a way to safeguard yourself ahead of time even before these things pop up in your life. Know where you stand, and be confident that you stand there for a reason. You have considered all your options and have made intelligent choices that are right for you. You are protecting yourself with forethought. Gotta look out for number one, you know.

From now on, when you are faced with peer pressure, you will already have the hard part figured out. You'll think, "No, I don't want a cigarette"—not because your parents and public service announcements told you not to smoke, but because you've already thought about it and decided that you don't want to be one of those people who blows all their money on something that's slowly killing them. You'll think, "No, I don't want to have sex yet"—not because of the lectures but because you've realized that you don't want the hassle of worrying about all the huge responsibilities that come along with it. It will be a lot harder to get talked into things when you know ahead of time that you're not interested. You've made your decisions, and you're sticking to your guns.

You want people to trust you—and when you make good choices, they will. Even if this means holding yourself back from the fun of the moment, you'll really have more freedom in the long run. Authority figures, such as parents and teachers, will leave you alone. They won't monitor your every move, and they won't tell you how to behave if they can trust that you will do the right thing on your own.

Steering Clear

Unfortunately, you can't always control your environment, no matter how hard you try. But you can control which environments you choose to hang out in. If a place has the potential to become uncomfortable, you probably want to stay away completely. By using this approach, you're pulling the peer pressure problem out by its roots.

But how do you tell ahead of time when a sweet party with your pals is gonna turn sour? You're no fortuneteller, and the Crystal Ball

Emporium in your town shut down last month. How are you supposed to be able to predict the future? Believe it or not, it is somewhat possible. If you know what to look for, you'll be able to spot a potentially shady situation from a mile away and avoid it ahead of time.

You need to learn how to identify the signs that point in an ugly direction so that you can steer clear and save yourself big trouble. The warning signs vary from situation to situation but are usually pretty obvious. For instance, "keg," "bong," and "abandoned crack den" are buzzwords for trouble. All you have to do is pay attention to what's going on around you. There will always be surprises, but at least you'll have done all you can to be on top of things.

Pressure Cooker

Fight cluelessness! There's nothing more dangerous than floating along in your own little bubble. When you don't pay attention, you're not contributing to the decisions being made by the group. When you snap out of it, you could find yourself somewhere you would have never decided to go on your own.

Be aware of who you are with and what they're into. Even if you're hanging with new friends, you probably have an idea of what they like to do for fun. Do they dig a night at the batting cages like you do? Or would they rather spend their night playing baseball with the neighborhood mailboxes? Think about this and decide whether you want to be a part of it. If your pals are troublemakers, you'll be joining their trouble. Of course, there's always the chance that the night will be innocent, but decide whether you even want to take that risk. It's easier to just keep your distance than to walk into a situation that you won't be able to crawl out of later.

Always know where you are and where you plan on going. Make sure that the place isn't dangerous or off-limits in any way. Are you trespassing? Are you in a house unsupervised by adults? Are you fooling around near a highway or train tracks? When the location itself is against the rules, you're already in deep regardless of what you're actually doing there.

Now, think about the activity you and your chums are about to take part in. Consider whether your actions would break a law or a rule or would get you in any trouble. Is it a bad move? Could it seem innocent at first but potentially become a bummer scene? Let's say that you hear that Scotty Stoner is having a raging party at his house because Mom and Pop Stoner are out of town. You're sure that Spicy Suzy will be there, and you've been waiting for an opportunity to hang out with her outside school. But, you know what Scotty and his buds are into: bud. You know there's going to be pot all over this shindig. That's a bad scene, kiddo. You're better off making other plans. Don't worry, Suzy's not going anywhere. There will be plenty of better times to make your move, in plenty of better places.

You may do a great job of playing Danger Watchdog, but sometimes you just can't help being caught off-guard. You considered the situation before you got into it, and everything seemed a-okay. There was no mention earlier of what was going to go down, but now things have taken a different turn, and you're not sure you like the direction. You have a bad feeling, but you can't really put a finger on it. Listen carefully to the other teens you're with. Pick out any hints of shady things to come. If you hear something fishy or just sense it, take off or get prepared to deal.

Situations are not always easy to read. It may be hard to tell whether it's cool. If a scene is borderline, consider your options. Usually you have only two: Do it or don't do it. That sounds simple, but it is often a difficult decision to make. Make a quick list in your head of pros and cons. This can help steer you in the right direction. If the bad outweighs the good—and it usually does—you've answered your own question. Do the smart thing and back off!

You have to judge situations for yourself. When others are pressuring you, they tell you only what they want you to hear. They will mention the good stuff and will conveniently avoid what could go wrong. After all, if you knew the truth, they'd have a way harder time convincing you. Besides, they're trying to ignore that stuff, too. It's no fun to think about the negative side of your actions— that's a total buzz kill. They would rather just continue on trying to have what they foolishly believe is a good time.

Kids with a Clue

"I was supposed to see a movie with some of my friends. When I got there, they were talking about sneaking in without paying. Instead of maybe getting busted, I just left. The whole thing was so stupid."

—Maya, age 14

Don't fall into the same trap of denial. You're only kidding yourself. That weakens your defenses and allows you to live in a total fantasy world. Be real and be honest. Even if it seems like it would be more fun and less hassle to just go along with the activity, it's probably a bad idea in the long run. You may be laughing now, but you'll be crying later.

When you decide how to handle the situation, do it. Either back out or jump in. But do it willfully. State your case firmly, and don't waver. Peers who pressure will see that you are fluctuating and will pounce. It looks to them like you're not sure about the choice you made and that you're still convincible.

Remember, think about the situation you're walking into before you do anything. Ask yourself these questions:

- What are these other teens into that I'm not? Drugs? Drinking? Vandalism?
- If they start doing this stuff, how will I feel?
- Is the place we're going to hang out off-limits anyway?

- Could anything we might do get us in trouble?
- Is it worth the risk?

If you don't like your answers to these questions, stay away. Let the others do what they want to do without you. You'll save yourself plenty of trouble. And you barely had to get your hands dirty.

Tactics, Excuses, and Lies: The Trilogy

You want freedom from your parents, from school, and from all the rules that you feel restrict you like an itchy woolen straightjacket that you can't get out of. You resist authority, or think about resisting, all the time. You don't want to be controlled by anything or anyone. Then why-oh-why do you allow your peers to control you? That's exactly what happens every time you succumb to peer pressure. You are doing what someone else wants you to do instead of what *you* want to do. It's a crazy contradiction when you think about it. When peers make you do something that you don't want to, it shows that they have power over you. Why should you allow them to be your boss? Aren't you trying to be your own boss? Stand up for yourself, and don't let anyone walk all over you—not the popular kids, not the older and bigger kids, and not even your girlfriend or best friend. Nobody.

Try as you may to avoid sticky situations, sometimes you will inevitably find yourself smack dab in the middle of some scary swamp of peer pressure, wishing you could disappear. Too bad your magic is a little rusty. You're in the mouth of danger, and you've got to take some kind of action to get yourself out of it.

The most simple, old-school method works like a charm: Say it loud and say it proud—"No!" If someone offers you a joint, say "No!" If someone asks to copy your homework, say "No!" If someone dares you to take off your clothes and streak down the main hallway at school during a fire drill, say "No!" Just because "No!" is typed here with an exclamation mark doesn't mean that you have to scream it. You don't have to be weirdly adamant or sound like a goody-goody when you pass on the offer. Just answer in the negative. Say

"Thanks anyway," and move on—unless, of course, the person continues to pressure you or pushes you harder. Then wear it on a sandwich board, say it in sign language, or yell it in a foreign tongue if you have to—anything to get the pressure off your back.

Kids with a Clue

"I went to a party where there were college kids and they were all getting high. My friends started smoking to look cool, but I passed. I said 'No, thanks' and went to the kitchen for some chips. It was easy."

—Billy, age 17

Let's say that you see a situation start to heat up, and you're not sure how to handle it. A good way to eliminate further discomfort or the chance of being faced with peer pressure that you don't need is to hightail it outta there. Just take off, exit, scram. If you're hanging out with a group, you can probably even slip away unnoticed. Make a great escape, smoothly and quickly. There's no telling what could happen if you stick around much longer. You may know what you want to do and are feeling pretty tough now, but if you let the others continue to bug you, your confidence could be shaken and your resistance may get worn down. Next thing you know, you could be giving in to something even though you thought you were in the clear.

If peers are trying to get you to do something that you're just not into, try switching gears. A simple change of subject could totally shift things away from the crappy direction they were headed. Teenagers are easily distracted. They have so much on their minds and are constantly turning their heads so that they don't miss anything. It can often be easy to move them onto a different path. This will throw them off, and they could totally forget what they were just saying to you. Pick a topic that you know they'd like to talk about, and run with it. If Creepy Chris says to you, "Do you want to take my dad's car for a spin? He'll never know," you can say, "Hey Creepster, whatever happened to that ant farm you were raising?" He'll probably start rambling and forget all about what he was just trying to convince you of in the first place.

You can also get yourself out of hot water by suggesting a different activity. You're young and you're fun. There are plenty of ways to occupy your time. Even the kids who try to push you into bad stuff are usually up for a change of pace. Think of a good alternative. Try to figure out something else that you both would be into doing. Rebel Roxie might suggest, "What do you say we go get a six-pack and hang out with those senior cuties behind the old factory?" You could answer, "Hey, Rebelita, I've got a better idea. Let's go play with Mojo, your 6-foot-long pet iguana, instead. I love that lizard." Roxie lives for him and loves when she can get one of her friends to actually go near the thing. And you're off, headed to her pad and away from the wack scene back at the factory.

You're dreaming of your grown-up days to come, but, face it: Sometimes acting like a kid feels refreshing. When used correctly, childish tactics can help you resist peer pressure. Just try the old ignoring trick. If someone is squeezing you into a corner and it's making you claustrophobic, try acting like they're not there. Mullet Mike might say, "Take a hit of this. It'll rock your world." You say " . " That's right—say nothing. He may ask again, but just say the same nothing. He'll eventually get bored and move on to someone or something else. Nobody likes to feel like he's talking to a wall. Besides, it looks kind of ridiculous. In moments, the Mullet Man will probably run his fingers nervously through his hair and get out of yours.

Another way to reach safe ground when being pressured is to talk yourself out of the jam. You can talk. Boy, can you talk, sometimes even too much, which someone has probably told you at one time or another. Even the shyest, quietest teens have a whole dialogue going on in their minds constantly. Use that gift of gab for a good purpose. Make up an excuse about why you can't do the lame thing you're being pressured into. Loopy Lucy might say to you, "I bet I can steal more candy from Choo-Choo's Choco-shop than you can." You say, "Whoops, Luce! I totally forgot, I told my mom I'd help her weed the garden." Or, you might say, "Holy canolli! I have to get home before curfew or I'll be grounded for life!"

When the teen piling on the pressure is a friend of yours, you can use that fact to your advantage to get yourself out of trouble. Lay the old guilt trip on, and hopefully your friend will give it a rest. Shane the Pain might say, "I'm gonna tell my mom I'm sleeping at your house tonight even though I'm gonna hang with that Hottie Hannah. Okay with you?" You can say, "It's a shame, Shane, that you're passing me the blame. Then I could get busted, too. A real friend would never do such a thing." Shane will probably slink away, feeling like the tool he is. Maybe he'll even reevaluate the way he treats his pals.

Lying is a crappy thing to do to anyone, especially people you care about. Unfortunately, when peer pressure rears its scaly head, it can sometimes be your best defense. If you feel like you're drowning and you can't think of any other way to save yourself, just make something up. Sneaky Sandy might say, "Let's take a bottle out of my folks' liquor cabinet. They never touch the stuff." You can say, "I'm totally allergic to alcohol. I get all splotchy and my eyes bulge out. You'll end up picking my baby blues off your kitchen floor." You're deceiving her, true, but it got you out of a tough situation.

A great way to combat peer pressure is with the greatest weapon of all: laughter. No one can resist a good joke or a great sense of humor. Laughing is one of the best feelings in the world. A good belly laugh makes even the grouchiest cranks feel happy and content. It's a powerful secret weapon, and it works like a charm in most situations. Cracking a joke will lighten the mood and set others at ease. It can distract everyone's attention away from the matter at hand and get them rolling on the floor. No one can ignore a good one-liner. Or a clever quip. Or a self-deprecating comment. Or a funny voice. Or a contorted face. Or a fart joke, for goodness sake. When Larry the Lush starts passing out nitrous balloons at his party, you can say, "Ever since that bad experience at clown school, I haven't been able to touch the stuff." You're bound to get giggles from the group, and chances are good that they'll move on and away from you.

Showing Your Strength

Some peer-pressure incidents are more powerful and harder to deal with than others. Tough times call for tough lines. One of the gang you sit with at lunch might call you a chicken in front of everyone because you don't want to cut the next class with him. You feel put on the spot, but there's no reason why he should be in control of the situation. Flip it around on him and push him right back by fighting fire with fire. Say to him, "Obviously you don't want to cut by yourself. Sounds like you're the wimp."

Even though they may be your friends, teens who peer pressure other teens are flat-out bullies. Why not tell them so? "Are you, like, peer pressuring me right now? That is so lame. It's so after-school special. Get a life!"

When push comes to shove, you need to resort to anything you can to get yourself out of the trouble peer pressure is trying to suck you into. Scare tactics are a powerful way to stop peer pressure in its tracks. And, face it, sometimes the offender deserves it.

Kids with a Clue

"We were at a party and our driver got so wasted. She thought she was fine and tried to get behind the wheel. When I told her she couldn't wear her awesome prom dress if she was dead, she handed me the keys and we all got home safe."

—Kara, age 17

Even if they know that what they are doing is wrong and stupid, people hate to be reminded of that. They decide to do it anyway, for whatever warped reason their little minds have come up with. They'd like to just ignore the possible negative consequences, hang out, and have fun regardless of what it might mean later. You can always remind a peer about the possible repercussions of his actions. Tell him that he could really get busted—or hurt. It may just scare him into backing down. If someone is trying to push you into something like smoking, tell her that she's going to die a slow, miserable death at an early age. And to top that off, she'll have yellow teeth and bad breath along the way. That should shut her up for a second.

These are all shrewd tactics that will hopefully help you turn awkward situations around. They don't always do the trick easily, but they make a great launching pad. You also have to be a quick thinker. Get a logical plan together in your head that you'll be able to execute within seconds. Sometimes, you need a couple of comebacks to ward people off and get you out of a tight situation. Try combining tactics. If one doesn't work, be ready with a couple of others. It's a tough job, but everybody's got to do it.

In the end, there's no substitute for an intelligent, confident attitude. Be sure of yourself. Be a strong teenager and a strong person. People are attracted to this trait more than any other. You'll start to get a reputation as a positively cool force to be reckoned with. You always do what you want and don't let *anyone* push you around. And that is truly cool.

The Least You Need to Know

- Be an independent thinker. Develop your own educated ideas and attitudes about everything. When you know your opinions ahead of time, you will be more apt to stick by them in the face of peer pressure.

- The best way to avoid a tense peer pressure situation is to never get into it in the first place. Read the signs and learn to catch the warnings before they catch you off-guard.

- There are lots of ways to beat peer pressure at its own game. Learn some of them, and you'll be prepared and ready to resist.

- Sometimes, the pressure is put on you full-force and needs to be battled with all the strength you can muster. Stand tall and get ready to give villains a taste of their own medicine.

Chapter 10

A Gentle Push in the Right Direction

In This Chapter

- Creature comparisons
- We can all use a muse
- Take it to the limit
- The warm, fuzzy feeling of friendship

Peer pressure is a major force in the life of every teenager. It causes anxiety powerful enough to shake even the strongest wills. But have hope—everything has a flip side. The other end of the peer pressure spectrum is just as intense but in an incredibly positive way. Yes, peer pressure can be as good as it is bad. You can take advantage of the good stuff if you are open to it, so learn to filter out the junk and let the sun shine in!

Healthy Competition

Peer pressure is a mean, rotten, smelly monster with dirt under its fingernails, bugs in its teeth, and permanent morning breath. Well, at least, that's the picture of peer pressure that we've painted so far. That monster has hidden under our beds and given us all nightmares at one time or another. We've stressed out and freaked out, felt left out and pushed in. We've suffered butterflies in the stomach, weak knees, and sweaty palms. The situations that we confront are never as easy to deal with as we hope. But we do it, manned with our guts, our nerve, and a few tricks up the sleeves of our jean jackets.

The good news is that the peer pressure beast has a twin—fortunately, not an identical one. His doppelganger is similar, but without all the warts. The alter ego of negative peer pressure is … drum roll, please … positive peer pressure! It's true, this awful annoyance does have a brighter side that is not only prettier, but also helpful and productive.

You may be wondering how pressure of any kind can be considered good. True, pressure is damaging when it forces you to do something that you don't want to, especially when that thing is dangerous, unlawful, or against your morals. But pressure does not have to be a vice grip that squeezes so tight that it feels like you're caught in a strangle hold. It can be gentle and as simple as a soft nudge that is just enough to sway you in a direction that you wouldn't think to go. Sometimes, you get lucky and are pushed uphill instead of down.

As you already know, relationships with peers serve many purposes, one of which is the constant opportunity for comparison. This can be detrimental if a teen goes overboard, obsessing over how everyone else looks and acts when he should instead be concentrating more on himself. However, when viewed with clear eyes, this comparison can be the on-ramp to the highway to higher ground.

Watching everyone else's every step all the time is enough to shake even the healthiest ego. "Am I as pretty as she is?" "Why did he score a half-grade higher on his test than I did?" "How will I ever make the team if I'm up against them?" Paying too much attention to how and what your peers are doing can work your nerves and launch you head-first into the clouds of uncertainty and insecurity. It's unfair and pretty impossible for you to make an accurate assessment anyway. After all, you are an involved party who has enough emotional and hormonal surges to deal with. You don't need the added pressure of voluntarily entering yourself into imaginary contests with your peers. But you do it regardless, and you do it all the time.

Vice Advice

Teens are notoriously hard on themselves. But give it a rest. Try looking at yourself with a fresh perspective. You will find that the person you see is way more amazing than you ever noticed before.

Try to keep your comparisons to a minimum, but don't stop paying attention altogether. It's important to know about the great things other teens are doing. You do want to stay on top of that, don't you? You want to keep up with them, and you want to do great things, too.

As the saying goes, "A little healthy competition never hurt anyone," and it's true. Healthy competition can be a wonderful thing—with emphasis on the word *healthy*. In this case, *healthy* means "moderate" and is a means to a positive end. Again, let's review: Going overboard is never a smart idea.

Competition in its extreme form is as old as time. Cavemen had to struggle to survive, and only the strong did. They had to be bigger, smarter, and tougher than their neighbor just so that they could get some prehistoric pot roast to bring home to their cave wives. It was a bloody time, and there is definitely some of that residual nastiness left around today. The cutthroat attitude has been known to bring down entire countries and break up great loves, so beware and keep that competitive nature in check.

However, the competitive bug can bite and not necessarily be poisonous. It can act as a catalyst, pushing you to do a better job. You want to be a part of the group, and you want people to think highly of you. You watch what the others are doing and make sure that you're doing the same thing they are—and doing it equally as well.

Competition is a constant presence among intellectually minded students. Performance in class becomes almost a game in which the players work as hard as they can to do as well, if not better, than their peers. High test scores, a quick working pace, and ability to solve even the most difficult problems become goals, even if they never were before, just in an attempt to show up classmates. The student hopes that along with success comes the admiration of her brainy peers. Sometimes, a student is an underachiever or is just plain lazy, but she is urged to push herself harder in an effort to keep up with her friends. Eventually, she is playing the Brain Game and working at this accelerated pace all the time. She is getting closer to reaching her own potential. She would never have gotten to such a level had she not felt a little friendly competition with her peers.

Kids with a Clue

"I've always been good at baseball even back in Little League. Then I met Dan, and he was so much better than me. I worked my butt off just to get as good as him. Now, we're pretty much the same, but I watch him at practice to make sure we stay that way."

—Jayson, age 15

A sense of competition can be felt in many other aspects of teen life. The positive push also nudges quite forcefully in athletics.

Sports are competitive by nature, so it's no surprise that the field and court play home to many types of contests, both official and unspoken. Often the people who end up being rivals are those with a similar level of skill. These battles are usually a close race, with the players pushing as hard as they can to make it to the finish line first. In the wide world of sports, teens strive for excellence in an attempt to not only measure up but also surpass the talents of the others. A good dose of healthy competition muscles you into pushing the boundaries of what you're physically capable of. It can show you how to achieve greatness that you may never have known possible.

A Guiding Light

You spend a lot of time with your pals and classmates—a lot. Whether you're hanging in the hallways, are heading out on the town, or are kickin' it at one of your houses, you're around each other for hours at a time. Your friends are your home away from home—they're supportive and they get you. However, even though you're a part of the same group and have some similarities, you are all very different. Sometimes, you feel so different that you wonder how you can even be friends at all.

But somehow it works. These differences make you a unique individual. You should revel in the details that make you your own person. They keep life interesting. But these quirks and varied interests serve another important purpose, one that friends should thank each other for. Whether you notice it or not, you are contributing something very valuable to the lives of your buds. You are a source of inspiration to them, and they move you, too.

You're a teenager now, and you're feeling pretty grown-up. You're maturing, and you understand life better than ever before. It's still like a giant puzzle, but you've got more of the pieces put in now. But even though you are soaking everything in and are way ahead of where you were even a couple of short years ago, you've barely seen the tip of the iceberg. There is an entire universe out there with an infinite amount of information just waiting to be discovered.

You live in a house filled with people who love you. They teach you things, both by guidance and by example. Back in your younger days, your primary—and pretty much only—influence was your parents. You knew about only things that your family taught you. If your dad liked do-wop music from the 1950s, that's what you grooved to as well. If your mom liked to watch baseball on TV, you probably sat with her to cheer on the boys of summer. The same thing is true of extended family and family friends. When you were little, your life revolved around these people. Your world ended at your front door, and everything beyond that was your concern only when you were allowed to go out and play.

As you got older, you made friends outside your home, probably when exploring the brave new world of your neighborhood. When you were old enough to start school, you were around lots of other kids. You had known some before, but never this many, never all in one place, and certainly never for so many hours a day. It was sensory overload of the best kind. Everything suddenly changed, and the focus of your whole life started to shift.

You began to branch out of the house and into your own social life. Now, you have your peers to learn things from. Think about it: They also grew up in homes with families that had lots of different interests that rubbed off on them, just like your family did with you. They come from different backgrounds with different influences, and they've had different experiences. Teens develop their own style and tastes in all different areas: music, art, clothes, sports, and so on. And each of us has a unique personality, to boot. With each person you meet, each teen you know, and each friend you make, you are exposed to all of another person's details—and that person is exposed to yours. Your world is expanding, and you are, too—even if you're too wrapped up in it to notice.

It's not that your friend sits you down and says, "Let me teach you about astronomy," but he may have invited you over to show you the telescope that he and his dad use for star-gazing. You never thought much about it before, but since that night, you find yourself looking up at the sky and picking out the North Star. You realize that you wouldn't mind knowing a little more about the Big Dipper, so you take a book out of the library and read up on it. Your friend was inspired by his dad, and you were inspired by him.

Maybe you've just started hanging out with a new bunch of friends who are totally into skateboarding. You've never really gotten on a board before, but you like these guys, so you figure that you'll give it a try. Even though they've never said anything that made you feel left out, and they probably never would because they're totally cool, you feel the force of some peer pressure. You're going to give skateboarding a shot so that you can fit in better with this new group. The worst thing that can happen is that you fall, skin your knee, scare your mom, and swear off wheels forever. The best-case scenario is that you try it and actually like it. No matter what, you've totally benefited because you were exposed to something new and gave it a shot. It was a valuable experience, and someday you can tell your grandkids about the week you tried to be Skater Dude.

Inspiration is a valuable thing, so find it where you can. Pay attention to what your peers are into and get used to testing things out. You never know what might strike your fancy. It's really hard to tell at first glance, so give everything a chance. If you're not thrilled after you try something, at least you know for a fact that it's not your bag. After all, you can't insist that you hate green olives if you've never tasted them. You could be missing out on the great passion of your life.

Kids with a Clue

"My friend Cassie learned how to crochet from her mom. I always thought it was something old people did, but when I saw the awesome blanket she made, I had to learn, too. Now, we crochet together while we talk about boys and stuff."

—Brooke, age 16

The Need to Succeed

You're not quite an adult yet, but you definitely feel that you've moved beyond kid-dom. The problem is that you're not really thrilled with being treated like either one although you're pretty sure that most days you would rather curve your age up than down. You constantly struggle to get everybody to trust you and treat you like the mature individual you are—or, at least, try to be. Sometimes, it feels like everything you do is really just an attempt to act older, cooler, or better so that people will take you more seriously. And whether you're into reading the business section of the newspaper or you flip right to the funny pages, you still deserve to be treated with respect.

Unfortunately, this does not always happen. Your Aunt Delilah might still pat you on the head and talk to you in a cutesy baby-waby voice. Even though she is a little wacky and always smells like pickles, it's annoying. At school, the same kind of stuff probably happens. Just because you're kind of quiet in class does not mean that you're invisible. You would think that Mr. Martin, your shop teacher, would have gotten that by now and made the effort to memorize your name instead of always referring to you as "Hey, you." After all, you have been in his class for six months already, and you don't call him "Mr. Nine-and-a-Half Fingers." Fair or not, these things happen, and you're sick of it.

You want to be noticed, and you want people to think about you. It's partly for the attention, but it's also because you want some acknowledgment. You want to count, and you want to be considered an important person. But how are you supposed to win people over when they all seem so wrapped up in their own stuff and can hardly be bothered by anything that doesn't affect them personally?

You've made a lot of attempts and tried lots of methods to get people to turn their heads. Some of your tries have been great efforts, while others have been just futile grasps at straws. Speaking in a loud voice seemed like a good idea until you started to annoy everyone, including yourself. Misbehaving seemed to work for other kids, so you tried that, too. It was working like a charm, and people paid attention, all right. Too bad you were grounded all the time and couldn't even enjoy your notoriety.

Pressure Cooker

Some teens are so desperate for attention that they go to extreme measure just to get noticed. These daredevils risk their own safety and sometimes the safety of others for those 15 minutes of fame.

You're ready to try anything now. Once, the thought actually crossed your mind of running onto the football field during the homecoming game and tap dancing wearing a clown wig and a tutu. Everyone would definitely notice, they'd laugh, and you would all bond over the fact that you're quite a character. Finally, you would get some attention. Needless to say, you chickened out at the last minute and tried to inconspicuously hide the rainbow curls under your baseball cap. You have to come up with something better, fast. You're not digging this invisible thing. You're a real almost-grown-up person, and you deserve a little r-e-s-p-e-c-t.

You need a different plan, something that's simple but effective. You've tried everything—being loud, being bad, being funny. There's only one thing left. How about being good for a change? Sounds crazy, but it just might work.

Excelling at something will move you to the head of the class, in front of all the teens who make you feel like you're lagging behind or fading into the background. It will make you shine, proving to others that you are a strong enough, smart enough, good enough person who is more than capable of making it to the top of the heap. You will be set apart and will no longer be a needle in the giant haystack of high school.

Because you are so aware of what your peers are up to, you are constantly reminded of their achievements. Lee went mountain climbing last summer, Brian is probably going to be valedictorian, and

Stacy got cast in a play at the local theater. No one says anything, but in your mind you hear them ask, "What have you done lately that makes you special?" "Why should we be friends with you?" "What are you going to do that will make us think that you're worth our precious time?"

If you're not sure of where your strengths lie, start exploring some untraveled roads. Become more adventurous, and you're bound to find something that you'll be good at and actually enjoy. You will soon discover that you're working hard to excel at your new passion. Undoubtedly, this will garner you some attention and the pats on the back that you've been yearning for.

When your achievements are noted and you receive praise, even if it's only a simple smile or a compliment, you will try hard to receive this kind of attention again. Face it, it feels good to be told that you're doing a great job whether you're writing a sonnet or simply mowing the lawn. Just like when you were a little tyke, you want others to look at you and think, "Boy, that kid's swell."

If you see other teens do something well and get complimented, you will want to do the same. Let's say that your best friend starts a rock band and everyone thinks she's cool for doing it. Now you feel like you should start one, too, but you are totally tone-deaf and don't know your maracas from your Mozart. Her actions will encourage you to find something that you rock at, and you'll dive right in.

Receiving attention and praise makes you feel like whistling and walking through a garden in slow motion with birds on your shoulders and squirrels at your feet. It's that feeling that keeps you coming back for more. It's addictive and especially valuable at this time in your life when you're unsure which end is up. You're figuring out who you are, and your accomplishments help you do that. You're beginning to feel more like a whole person. These goals that you achieve build your confidence. Your self-esteem gets a boost as well because you are learning the extent of your potential. And the mind-blowing part is that your potential is endless! Whether you're pushing yourself because you long for the approval of others or just because you want to get noticed, go for it. Every step makes you a stronger, richer, more fulfilled person. And you're only getting better.

Golden Friends Are Priceless

No one ever said that growing up would be easy. Actually, no one ever really said much about it to you at all. You had to figure it out for yourself, and you're still working on it. It might not always be fun, but you're getting by—somehow. But wouldn't it be nice if there was some kind of guidebook to help you get through? A map would come in handy, one that warned you if a river was too deep to cross and which bridges have dragons hiding underneath. Sadly, no such book or map exists because the journey varies so much from person to person. At least the teen years should have come with a warning label: Proceed with Extreme Caution! Then you could have strapped on your armor and been a little more prepared.

You've got your armor on now, though. It may have taken you a while to figure out how to protect yourself, but you eventually got it. Hopefully, you're feeling a little safer than at the start of your trip. You have now developed an attitude and a personality that seem to be working pretty well for you. Maybe you've thrown in a touch of sarcasm for good measure. You'll need all of it because issues with your peers can feel way bigger, way more important, and way more dangerous than anything you've ever imagined. You need a little help from your friends to get you through.

All this would be a lot simpler if true friends were easy to find. Good friends provide a shoulder to cry on and someone to count on. They are great dispensers of unconditional respect and love. Who wouldn't want one? But you can't just order up the perfect friend. There's no Super Friend Mart out there where you can just toss one in your cart with a pack of donuts and whisk through the express checkout. Truly healthy, vibrant friendships are not common, but they are possible when cultivated with care.

Before you can enjoy a great friendship, you must learn how to identify a good friend. You probably call a bunch of people your friends. You hang out together, have stuff in common, and have fun. But some people don't hold up their end of the bargain. Some of them might even make you feel bad sometimes. Maybe they are catty, tease a lot, or put others down. Have you ever been on the receiving end of their harsh words? They might have tried to pass it off as just kidding around. They might have turned it on you and told you to stop being so sensitive. But you can tell whether it's a joke: If your feelings were hurt, that's no joke. And that's no friend.

Real friends do some important things:

- Listen to each other.
- Support each other in everything they do.
- Don't make judgments.
- Stand up for each other, even when others are against them.
- Are loyal.
- Are there for each other.
- Can trust each other.
- Have mutual respect.
- Are happiest when they can be themselves and when others are genuine, too.
- Like each other for who they are.

Think about each of your friends for a minute. How many of them do all of these things? Probably not many. Some of them may even pressure you to do stuff that you don't want to do. A real friend would never do a thing like that. They can be okay people—they're just not true friends. You can keep them around for laughs, but be careful and be aware that they don't treat you the way you deserve to be treated. They are fair-weather friends who will hop a bus out of town at the first sign of rain.

Kids with a Clue

"I used to feel like I had to be friends with the whole school, so I was. I still felt totally alone. Then, I just started hanging out with the people I really liked. Now, even though I have only a few good friends, I'm way happier."

—Melissa, age 14

What about those friends of yours who do all the things on that list and do them well? Those are the people you need to hold on to because they will always be by your side. But to make and keep good friends, you need to be a good friend yourself.

Consider yourself for a moment. Look inside and really think about how you treat others. How do you measure up according to the list? Be honest with yourself; if you know that you could use some improvement, make the change. Work on these things, and you will be a better friend to others and a better person for you.

The Least You Need to Know

- Although a severely competitive nature often leads to the destruction of a friendship, a little friendly competition can provide a much-needed push to excel.

- The hobbies and interests of your peers can influence you to develop your own and can provide inspiration that will enrich your world.

- Teenagers have a strong need to do well in everything they try. This need to achieve makes them want to work harder to be the best, to win the admiration and approval of others.

- Good friends are hard to find, but when you do find one, you will have a friend for life. Remember, being a good friend attracts good friends.

11

Expert Advice: Getting It, Giving It, and Coming Out on Top

In This Chapter

- Getting it off your chest
- Coaching your contemporaries
- Rockin' role models
- You'll laugh about this later

At this point, you should pretty much consider yourself an expert on peer pressure. You know what it is, when it happens, and how to confront it. In this chapter, we explore the options teens have when the pressure becomes too much to handle on their own. We'll tell you how and where to get help, and we'll show you some great ways that you can mentor others who need a little guidance. It's important to keep a healthy attitude and remember that no problem is too big to deal with.

Talking Your Troubles Away

Sometimes, the problems that you face are just too overwhelming to tackle by yourself. You need some helpful hints—lucky for you, your friends are right there. They are experiencing the same growing pains that you are and can be the perfect leaning post when you're feeling down and out. However, at other times, their love and support just aren't enough. Sometimes, you feel the serious stress really mounting up. Other times, you have bigger problems that even they don't know how to coach you through. Or maybe you've got something on your mind that you want to keep private, and you don't feel comfortable sharing it with your buds. Fortunately, there are many good options and directions to turn to for some solid advice. You just have to know where to look.

The obvious first choice is in your own backyard. You can run your dilemma by your parents. We know that you probably just let out a single sarcastic "Ha!" and thought about how you'd rather chew glass. But think about it: They love you unconditionally, and the last thing they want is to see you suffer. They also might surprise you. They are older, and, believe it or not, wiser; they also are able to see things with a clearer head. It may be hard to believe, but they were your age once, and although times have changed, they dealt with similar issues back in the Stone Age of their adolescence. Even though you feel like they don't understand you, they do know you pretty well—technically, since before you were born, which is way longer than anyone else. That's got to count for something.

But what if your folks are your problem? Approaching them for a neutral opinion is not happening. If you are fortunate enough to have older siblings, they can be the perfect solution. They live in the same house. They understand the dynamics better than anyone on the outside can. Maybe they've already "been there, done that" with the issue troubling you and can tell you how to solve it. Either way, they are a great sounding board because they have front-row seats and a soft spot for all the players.

Unfortunately, sometimes relatives are just not an option. You have something going on in your life that is better left outside the nest. A good place to turn for some guidance is … ahem … the guidance counselors at school. While most students utilize them mainly for their help in scheduling classes and getting through college applications, they are also there to serve another purpose: to help you get through these tough peer pressure–filled years with the fewest battle wounds possible. Guidance counselors are specialists in the field of adolescent anxiety and have heard almost everything. So, if you've got a real doozy, you might want to skip lunch one day and spill your guts in that cluttered little office. It might just do the trick.

Vice Advice

Getting your troubles off your chest will give you a huge sense of relief. When you don't feel like talking to anyone, try writing down everything that's bugging you. Pouring your heart out on paper can take a load off your mind.

Besides getting advice at school, you can turn in other directions. Any adult you trust would probably be willing to lend an ear. Try talking to your clergy, a family friend, or a trusted neighbor.

Another alternative is to see a therapist. These are specialists who are well trained to understand your problems and bestow expert advice. Therapy has become a more widely accepted and encouraged form of help than ever. It can be an amazing way to clear your head and vent your frustrations to somebody who is completely unbiased and out of your loop.

Some people still have a really old-fashioned view of therapy and think that only crazy people get comfy on that couch. You may think so, too, but that is *so* not the case. Therapists are professionals whose job is to listen to problems of all sizes, big and small. You might be afraid that if people at school find out you're talking to a therapist, they would think you were nuttier than a squirrel. Peer pressure rears its ugly head. You're convinced that you would be teased and get a reputation as a total psychotic. Before using this an excuse not to get yourself help, remember that the only way people will know you are in therapy is if you tell them. Some of your friends probably see shrinks right now, and you have no clue. Although it definitely matters what your friends think, you need to focus on your own problems and make yourself feel better. Forget about everyone else, and concentrate on the most important person in your life: you.

You might fear that a therapist will tell your parents everything you say. If they spill your secrets, your folks will find out some juicy details that are so none of their business. Well, stop panicking, because whatever you confide in your therapist is completely confidential. He can't tell your mom anything, no matter how much she begs. There are only a few times when your secret might not be safe. If your health or safety or the safety of someone else is at risk, the therapist will report it to your parents or the authorities. This is done only in extreme situations. Everything else is sacred. You can unburden yourself and be confident that the information stays within the confines of those four walls.

What if you want to see a therapist, but you've heard that they charge a jillion dollars an hour and there is no way your family can afford it? It's true that psychiatrists are notoriously expensive, but there are plenty of ways to get around that. You can talk to a psychologist, who does the exact same job but doesn't prescribe medicine. Social workers and counselors also are excellently trained and cost little or no money. No matter what your financial situation is, if you want to see a shrink, there's always a way to swing it.

As wonderful as therapy could potentially be, it doesn't work for everyone. You might have heard from a classmate that all it does is make you feel worse. If you believe that, then wild horses couldn't drag you there. The whole point is to stop feeling crappy, so why in the world would you subject yourself to something that will only intensify the suckiness of you life? While it's true that analysis makes you delve into some emotions that aren't the most pleasant, you have to realize that the therapist is right beside you, to make sure you'll be okay. You are being forced to confront your problems head on, and while that is definitely a challenge, it's better for you in the long run. After all, you don't want to bury your anger; it is only bound to resurface eventually.

Kids with a Clue

"My boyfriend broke up with me, and I was crushed. Instead of talking about it, I just ignored it. Two months later, he started dating this other girl and I totally flipped out and needed to see a shrink."

—Jessica, 17

Seeing a therapist seems worth a try, but how do you go about finding one? You could always crack open the Yellow Pages and flip to "Mental Health." You can ask your doctor if he can recommend anyone. After all, you trust him to make you better when you're sick, so take his advice on who he thinks can make your head feel better. Also, if you're comfortable, you can ask your friends or relatives who they suggest. They know your personality and might know a therapist who would be a perfect match for you. You could also call the psych department at a local college. The students are always eager to put their newly acquired skills to use, and they work for free.

Remember, finding the right professional is important. You might feel completely at ease on the first couch you lie down on. The process of choosing a therapist is a lot like dating and could take some time, so don't feel pressured into working with one just because you met him first. You may have to try on a few before finding one that fits. Don't let yourself get discouraged if it takes you a while, either. After all, most people don't wind up married to their grade-school sweetheart. Ask yourself these questions before investing time and money in an expert:

- Am I comfortable with the therapist?
- If not, is it because I'm uneasy about therapy or apprehensive of the therapist?

- Do I feel like she's really hearing me, or is she just listening to what I'm saying?

- Does she push for me to figure out you're my own solutions, or does she give all the answers?

It might be hard to instantly confide in a total stranger, but trust your instincts. If you sense that she gets it and can help you, give her a shot. But be wary of anybody who says that he knows exactly how you should solve your problems. Therapy is supposed to help you find your *own* way to deal with life and all of its bumps and bruises.

Therapists are not coddling. You aren't shelling out the dough to have somebody tell you exactly what you want to hear. Your sessions are to force you to confront the stuff in your life that makes you want to hide in a fort built with chairs and blankets. So be honest. Don't lie about how you feel or what you think because you are afraid that your therapist won't like you. Who cares if she does? She's paid to help you, not be your buddy. Be straightforward and tell it like is. A therapist needs to know the truth, the whole truth, and nothing but the truth, so give it to her.

Therapy is not a one-shot deal. It takes more than a single visit to get down and dirty with your problems. If your stuff was so easily solvable, you probably wouldn't have gone in the first place. When you decide to take the plunge, ride the wave for a while and give yourself a chance to let it work.

Teens Helping Teens

Sometimes, you crave conversation with another teen, and for what-ever reason, your buddies are just not right for the job. Many schools have special programs where students give support, encour-agement, and academic guidance to their fellow classmates. The goal is to offer comfort and information to teens who are struggling with the constant pressures of growing up and the feeling that the world is spinning so fast that you can't feel the ground.

You know those days when you wake up in the morning and every-thing is just a disaster? Your hair is screaming for a "hat day," your skin looks like something out of a horror movie, and the only way your jeans are closing is if you lie down, suck in, and worry about breathing out later. Forget the fact that you have two tests that you didn't study for and had a whopper of a fight the night before with your best friend. The pressure is suffocating and way more than you'd ever want to handle. Much as you'd like to play sick and watch trashy talk shows all day, you can't hide forever. You have to move forward, and sometimes you could use a push.

Try talking to a peer counselor. These are students in your school who are trained to help you solve your problems. They learn how to really listen to everything and pick up on the subtle details. They know how to hear what you're saying even when you're not exactly sure what you mean. They are taught to show you what your options are and how to figure out which alternative is right for you.

Unlike therapists, peer counselors are your age and are living with the same dilemmas you are. This may make them easier for you to relate to. They know what it's like at your school and therefore have a better grasp of where you are coming from. They walk the same hallways and eat in the same lunchroom, so they understand the social structure and how hard it can be if you don't like your place in the pecking order.

Kids with a Clue

"My parents were getting divorced, and it was killing me. My friends thought I was totally overreacting—their parents were all split up, and it was no big deal. So I talked to this girl who's a peer counselor at school, and she really listened to me. She didn't make me feel like I was lame for crying over it at all."

—Melissa, age 14

The benefit of talking to a peer counselor over your friends is that a counselor will tell it to you like it is. Your pals might be afraid to say something that you don't want to hear, for fear that it will jeopardize your friendship. There is nothing personal at stake with a peer counselor. It is the counselor's job to get you over the rough spots. If he has to confront you with a not-so-pretty truth to help, he will do it.

Peer mediating is another great way to problem-solve. When kids at school just can't see eye to eye and insist on going to war, often they are thrown into the snake pits known as detention and suspension. If you say "black" and he says "white," and neither of you can agree on gray, sitting in a classroom after the final bell will accomplish nothing but a lame slap on the wrist. However, there is a way to reach a middle ground. Qualified peer mediators are trained to look at both sides of an argument and come up with a way for all parties to be happy. Mediators are students just like you who have no interest in power-tripping. So, if somebody drives you so crazy that you think about socking him every time he crosses your path, consider sitting down with a mediator to alleviate some of the stress. It takes a lot more energy to hate somebody than it does to just let it go.

Academic problems are addressable, too. You can't understand why 3x equals the square root of 11 pi, and it's driving you nuts. Well, before you drop out to juggle in a traveling circus, check to see if your school offers peer tutoring. Another student may be able to help you grasp those concepts that just won't sink in. Tutoring is usually done one-on-one, so your particular problem is immediately dealt with. Also, when the person doing the coaching is your own age, you might be more inclined to ask questions that you fear would make your teacher roll her eyes. If you have a class that is making you lose sleep and lose hope, get a tutor to explain it to you in your own language. Your grade will go up, and so will your confidence.

All these student programs are completely confidential. It is entirely up to the person getting the help whether the relationship is public knowledge. If you are shy about people knowing that you're talking to a counselor, keep it classified. If you don't want your friends to know that you're being tutored in bio, then let your newly acquired A be a mystery. There's no shame in admitting that you can't handle everything that's thrown at you, though. You're only human, and so is everyone else. So, if you need help, get it!

Setting an Example

Maybe you are one of the fortunate few who has peer pressure
pretty much under control. You've read all about it, and you know
how to identify it and how to deal with it. You've learned how to
handle the tension, and you feel confident that you can take on the
world. You refuse to let a little thing like stress slow you down.
Congratulations are in order. Reach around and pat yourself on the
back—this is truly an accomplishment.

Done patting? Excellent. Because now you have a really important
job: putting your strength to good use. Most teenagers are not as
confident as you are, and everyone can use some help sometimes.
The best way for you to guide your friends and classmates is to lead
by example. It's not always easy to say "no" to peer pressure, but it
is easier if you're not the only one saying no. If you're at a party and
everyone else is getting stoned, let the joint pass you by. When you
show your strength by rejecting the hit, you've showed everyone
around you that it's okay to turn it down. By doing that, you're giving your friends an out. They might have felt weird about being the
only one not taking a puff, but you leading the way makes it easier
for them to stand strong, too.

The power of setting a good example holds in any situation where
peer pressure comes sauntering in uninvited. For instance, if you are
not ready to have sex, be open and honest about it. Let your friends
know that it's totally cool to wait and that there is nothing wrong
with staying a virgin. If they hear that you are so sure of yourself,
they might gather the nerve to do the same. Your influence may
stop them from jumping into the backseat of a car and doing something that they will later regret.

If any after-school club piques your interest, show up and be heard.
Anybody can join, but it takes true dedication and commitment to
be really involved. If you're the type who's really good with money,
become the treasurer of the French Club. If you like planning
events, organize the next car wash fund-raiser. Pick your passion
and seize control so that you can make a difference. Not only will
you feel incredibly accomplished, but also people will be impressed
by your tenacity and attracted to your strength.

You can set a positive example by standing up for what you believe in social situations as well as political ones. If there's a cause that moves you, get behind it whole-heartedly. Maybe you're fighting to let that chick with the awesome kick be the punter on the football team. Or, it could be animal rights that gets your blood pumping. Whatever your issue is, throw yourself into it and let everyone else know that you're totally gung-ho. Perhaps, it will give them the strength and encouragement to join your cause—or even to go out and accomplish something great on their own.

Kids with a Clue

"I always get really upset every time I see homeless people. Since I couldn't invite them to live at my house, I started volunteering at a shelter after school. A few of my friends heard about it. Now, they volunteer there, too."

—Jared, age 16

We've already emphasized how influential peer counselors and mediators are. If you're feeling confident and together, exercise your power and become a peer leader yourself. You could rock someone else's world for the better. It doesn't matter whether you're valedictorian, captain of the football team, a member of the AV club, or a student who needs remedial math. You could have rich parents or live on the wrong side of the tracks. None of that factors in if you are totally devoted to helping out your classmates. Teens from every background and social group make great advisers. And if you feel like you've got a particular subject down pat, become a tutor. Nothing feels as good as helping somebody over a hurdle.

The concept behind being a leader and a role model is a simple one that can be traced back to some of your favorite childhood games. Remember Follow the Leader? Or how about Simon Says? What do these classics have in common? They're both about being the head honcho, the boss that everyone has to imitate. And you always wanted to be the leader, right? There are no stories about kids duking it out to be a follower. You first choice was to be the person in charge, so why should it be any different now? Take it upon yourself to be the strong, smart, kind, and powerful teen that the rest of your classmates want to emulate. After all, there's nothing better than being Simon.

Keeping It in Perspective

You may sometimes feel really grown-up, but it's still very early in your great journey of life. You have many years ahead to succeed, to fail, and to just live. Cut yourself some slack, relax, chill out, try to enjoy yourself, and remember to breathe. While it might not seem like it now, the teen years are a very small amount of time in your life span and will be over before you know it.

If the pressure of being a teenager becomes way too heavy for you to carry, remember that there are places you can go and people you can talk to. No matter how huge of a problem you have, you must keep in mind that there are always solutions, and you're never alone. Getting through them might not be easy and probably won't be fun, but there is a light at the end of the tunnel. As horrible as things sometimes seem, lashing out with violence toward yourself or others is never an option. Your problems are temporary, but death is not. Things can feel dark in the moment, and if you find yourself floundering, run for help. Talk to somebody, no matter how hard it may be for you. Once the final curtain falls on life, there are no encores.

Pressure Cooker

Some teens have a hard time expressing themselves. If you have a friend who is obviously struggling, pay attention to his off-handed remarks. If he mentions suicide or violence, even in passing, recognize this as a cry for help and get him some.

No matter how plagued you are by your dilemma of the moment, remember that life moves quickly—before you know it, you'll move on to something else. Think back to when you were a kid and you cried your eyes out because your parents wouldn't buy you the action figure that you wanted so badly. You thought that nothing could be worse. It sounds ridiculous now, doesn't it? Well, the same thing is true today. What you yearn for so desperately will probably be totally forgotten a month from now. Don't waste valuable time miserably moping over the cute girl in geometry who won't give you a second glance, the new video game system that you can't afford, or the popular crowd that just won't let you be a member.

Whatever mortifying predicament you find yourself in, years from now it will probably become an amusing anecdote to tell at a party. "Back in high school, I was trying to play it cool in front of my crush. I wasn't paying attention and I completely missed the stairs. I rolled all the way down, splitting my pants and my boxer shorts and giving a show to the hottie, my ex-girlfriend, and my buddies from the swim team." While this is enough to make you want to transfer schools when it happens, we promise that you will see the humor in it once you get some distance. Don't forget that you go to one school in one town in one state in one country. There's a whole world of people you haven't met yet who have humiliating stories just as bad as your own.

Your problems may seem ground-shaking, but none of them will lead to the end of the world. What seems vital today will be forgotten tomorrow, so don't worry about it so much.

The pressure that your peers put on you can feel as heavy as a ton of bricks. But it's all deal-able. You can get through all of it with your head held high by using the tricks that we taught you and having a good sense of humor and perspective.

You have to make tons of decisions daily: Should you study more? Have a cigarette? Laugh when they make fun of the class nerd? Take your dad's sports car for a secret spin? Before you jump into anything, stop and consider your options and their consequences before acting. Do the right thing, and you'll come out of your teen years virtually unscathed. You can keep your cool and still *be* cool if you play your cards right.

Life as a teen is complicated because of all the crazy things happening to your body and mind. Everyone your age is going through it, so give them a break. And give yourself one, too. With confidence, strength, and kindness, you can become Super-Teen, fighting peer pressure, insecurity, and obnoxious bullies in a single bound. And, we promise, you don't have to wear the cape.

The Least You Need to Know

- When your troubles become too much to handle, find someone to talk to. There are plenty of options out there. The right one is the one that makes you feel better.

- If friends can't help but you want advice from someone your own age, turn to a peer counselor, mediator, or tutor. They are going through the same things you are and are chock full of insight.

- Be the best you can be by standing up for what you believe in. Besides helping yourself, you will help others who are looking for a lead to follow.

- No matter how hard things seem, keep it all in perspective. You're growing up and will grow out of your problems, too. So hang out, hang on, and hang tough. You'll make it out of your teens a better person.

Check out other Complete Idiot's Guide® for Teens Books !

SPIRITUALITY

The Complete Idiot's Guide®
to Spirituality for Teens
ISBN: 002863926X

DATING

The Complete Idiot's Guide®
to Dating for Teens
ISBN: 0028639995

LOOKING GREAT

The Complete Idiot's Guide®
to Looking Great for Teens
ISBN: 0028639855

ALPHA

 Arts & Sciences Business & Personal Finance Computers & the Internet Family & Home Hobbies & Crafts Language Reference Health & Fitness Personal Enrichment Sports & Recreation   Teens

IDIOTSGUIDES.COM

Introducing a new
and different Web site

Millions of people love to learn through *The Complete Idiot's Guide*®
books. Discover the same pleasure online in **idiotsguides.com**–part
of The Learning Network.

Idiotsguides.com is a new and different Web site, where you can:

- Explore and download more than 150 fascinating and useful mini-guides–FREE! Print out or send to a friend.

- Share your own knowledge and experience as a mini-guide contributor.

- Join discussions with authors and exchange ideas with other lifelong learners.

- Read sample chapters from a vast library of *Complete Idiot's Guide*® books.

- Find out how to become an author.

- Check out upcoming book promotions and author signings.

- Purchase books through your favorite online retailer.

Learning for Fun. Learning for Life.

IDIOTSGUIDES.COM • LEARNINGNETWORK.COM